The
REGGIE
JACKSON
Story

Bill Libby

Lothrop, Lee & Shepard Company

A Division of William Morrow & Co., Inc.

New York

Title-page photograph: *Wide World Photos*

Printed in the United States of America.
First Edition   1   2   3   4   5   6   7   8   9   10

Library of Congress Cataloging in Publication Data
Libby, Bill.
   The Reggie Jackson story.

   Includes index.
   SUMMARY: A biography of the controversial baseball player who has led teams to five pennants and four World Series championships and who has been Most Valuable Player in two World Series and his own league.
   1. Jackson, Reggie—Juvenile literature.   2. Baseball players—United States—Biography—Juvenile literature.   [1. Jackson, Reggie.   2. Baseball players]
I. Title.
GV865.J32L5   796.357′092′4 [B] [92]   79-684
ISBN 0-688-41889-9   ISBN 0-688-51889-3 lib. bdg.

*This book is dedicated fondly to a true friend,
Marvin Schneider, his Dorothy, and their sons,
Martin, Steven, and Greg.*

ACKNOWLEDGMENTS

The author wishes to thank Reggie Jackson for all the friendship extended him and courtesies shown him throughout the years. He wishes to thank Reggie's manager, Matt Merola, for all his help over the years. He wishes to thank all of the players, managers, and other officials for their help, and all the writers and photographers who provided so much of the material for this book.

Contents

1

The Hero

Whatever else he is, Reggie Jackson is an awesome athlete. He stands six feet tall, and weighs 200 pounds. He is so thickly muscled he looks as if he is constructed with concrete slabs. Yet he has a sprinter's speed. He combines strength and speed as have few athletes in the history of baseball.

He has to be careful running because he has suffered from pulled muscles throughout his career, but he can run. He has to be careful swinging a bat because he has suffered from a bad back throughout his career, but he swings as hard as any player ever. He has weak eyes and wears glasses, but he sees well enough to hit a hard-thrown ball.

Left-handed, he also has an arm that can rifle a baseball like a bullet the length of the playing field and frequently throws out runners on the bases. But he is erratic in the field. With his glove, he makes hard catches and misses easy ones. He has led leagues in errors. Also strikeouts. Also assists. And home runs. And runs batted in.

He is the most spectacular performer in his sport today—and the most controversial, on and off the field. He is good-natured and loves to laugh and have a good time. He is extremely bright and well-spoken. Reporters will tell you he is the best interview in sports. He may give too many interviews. He may talk too much. He is outspoken and speaks freely in ways that often get him into trouble.

Because of this, some people do not like him even though they do not know him. In this book, you will get to know him as you have not before. He is not easy to know, but he is a fascinating fellow.

Because of the controversies that seem to follow him off the field, he has become controversial on the field. Some doubt that he is a great player, but he has one of the greatest records any player has achieved.

He has led teams to five pennants and four World Series championships, a rare feat. He has been Most Valuable Player in his league and he is the only player to have been MVP in two different World Series.

He hit his peak in 1977 when he carried his club through a come-from-behind stretch run to a pennant and decided the World Series with a spectacular, record home-run barrage.

Then, in 1978, he again proved himself the greatest of pressure players when he came through again and again in the clutch as his Yankees staged the greatest comeback in sports history, winning another pennant and going on to win another World Series. He was thirty-two years old and in his eleventh season in the major leagues.

Reginald Martinez Jackson was born on the 18th of May, 1946, in Wyncote, Pennsylvania, but reared in Cheltenham, which is a suburb of Philadelphia. Reggie had two older brothers, Joseph and James, an older sister, Dolores, and two younger sisters, Beverly and Tina.

When Reggie was four or five years old, his parents parted. They later divorced. At first, he, Joseph, and Beverly stayed with their father, while James, Dolores, and Tina went to live with their mother in Baltimore. Later, James came to live with their father, while Beverly went to live with their mother. So it wound up with the three boys with the father and the three girls with the mother.

Reggie's middle name is his father's first name,

Martinez. Reggie says, "Dad's a good old dude, and I got a lot of respect for him. He was and is a tailor and has worked hard all his life for a living. I give him what he wants and he doesn't have to work any more, but he wants to, and does.

"I don't remember saying the word 'mom' until I was thirteen or fourteen. I didn't even get to know my mother until I was seventeen or eighteen. I've gotten to know her by now and she's a great lady. I bought a house for her. I'm happy I've gotten to do some things for her. I'm sure she would have done for me if she could have.

"Whatever happened between her and Pop, it happens. People don't mean for marriages not to work. It's hard to understand when you're a kid, but you see how it is as you grow older. I'm sure she didn't want to leave half her family behind her. It's only as I've grown older that I've gotten to know half my sisters and brothers.

"We lived in a little apartment over the tailor shop. My dad left for work early and got home late. I got up and got dressed and got to school by myself. There was never much money or a lot of food in the house so I made do with very little breakfast or lunch. When he got home eight, nine, ten, eleven at night, we had dinner.

"Maybe we had soup and a sandwich. He always managed to get something to throw on the table. But there were no extras. We had to earn our way. I delivered newspapers. I delivered dry cleaning for him. A lot of mornings I got up early to put in a couple hours in his tailor shop before going to school. I put in a lot of hours a lot of nights there.

"If I asked him for a quarter to go to the movies, he always asked me what I'd done to earn it. If I wanted pocket money I had to bust my butt on the back of his truck to earn it. He gave me time off to play ball, but if I wasn't playing ball I had to work in his shop. It was hard, dirty work in a hot, sweaty shop. I played a lot of ball.

"My dad played semi-pro baseball and boxed a little. He got crippled in the Army. He got a lame leg out of World War Two. But he could fight crippled and he could play ball crippled and he could work crippled. He was hustling hard for a buck all the time I was growing up. He didn't have much time for me. He did what he had to do to see that we got fed and clothed. He saw that the rent was paid. And he saw that most of us got to college. He did what he had to do."

He didn't always do the right thing. He ran numbers and bootlegged liquor on the side, neither of which was legal. When you run numbers, you sell chances for a fortune. A person picks three numbers and hopes those will be the three that come up at the end of the day as the last three numbers of something like the betting total at the race track that day.

A person pays a dime or a dollar or some such sum and hopes to get rich. Numbers betting long has been big in neighborhoods where poor people hope to get rich. A struggling tailor may run numbers for money he needs for his family. He is paid by some syndicate of criminals. Caught, Mr. Jackson was condemned as a criminal and spent six months in jail when Reggie was seventeen or eighteen.

Reggie says, "My brother Joe really raised me. He was tough. He used to beat the heck out of me if I didn't do my chores at home. I had to wash the dishes and clean the house and rake the leaves. I'm grateful to him. He's responsible for me being the way I am. I keep a clean house. I can afford help, but if someone doesn't do it for me, I do it. It's got to be done.

"If Dad sent me to the store for something, he expected me to get it. He didn't want to know if it was raining or snowing or I had to hitch a ride or walk. He wanted me to bring back what I'd been sent for. He had a phrase: He didn't want to hear any 'ar-ray-boo'—any baloney in other words.

"I believe in that. If you've got something to do, do it. Don't make excuses why you can't do it. And do it right.

"When Dad was gone, Jim came to live with us. Just like Joe and Dad, Jim was tough on me, too. He saw that I did what I had to do. But I was a

14

tough kid. And I was bitter because my dad had been taken away from me. I didn't see why he had been hassled for doing what he had to do.

"When you don't have much, it doesn't seem so bad to steal so you can get something. That's the way it is in poor neighborhoods and that's why there's so much crime there. I didn't grow up in a poor neighborhood, but I was a poor kid in a rich neighborhood and I didn't have the things others had there.

"It was mostly a white neighborhood, but my dad didn't know what color was, so we didn't either. There wasn't much prejudice there and the black kids like me and my brothers grew up with white kids, played ball with them, often fought for them against other black kids.

"There were a lot of Jewish people there and my girl friend in high school was Jewish as well as white. I didn't know what prejudice was until I went to college and a coach told me I'd get in trouble if I didn't stop dating white girls. My wife was white and I still date white as well as black girls. My friends are white and black and all kinds of religions.

"I'm black and proud of it, but beyond that I just don't care about color. My father's people were from Latin America so I'm part Spanish and proud of that, too. I don't ask people what they are before I'm going to be good to them. I roomed with a white guy when I was with the A's and I didn't even think anything about it until some people made a big deal over it.

"I think if people didn't make a big deal about race and religion a lot of us could live together a lot easier without even thinking anything about it.

"I didn't get into trouble in school because we were black and they were white, but because we were poor and they were rich. Or seemed rich to us. They had things we didn't have and wished we did.

"One day some kid stole my lunch. Lunch? It was a box of pretzels. I told the teacher that if I didn't get it back I was gonna bust someone. One of the guys was smiling because he saw she wasn't going to do anything. He threw a nickel on the floor. So I grabbed him and shoved him up against a wall and I said, 'Boy, don't you know I might kill you?' And he got nervous and said, 'Man, don't you do that. Why you want to do that?' I said, 'Cause I'm crazy.'

"I wanted them to think I was because it made them scared of me. I wasn't so big when I first got to high school. I was small so I had to act tough and be tough to get by. I acted crazy a lot because it made people scared of me. I wouldn't let anyone outside of my family tell me what to do. I'm still that way. Too much that way. I wish I wasn't. But I grew up acting tough and not letting anyone tell me what to do and doing what I wanted to do and it's sort of like a bad habit you can't break.

16

The Hero

"In her class one day, a teacher told my girl friend, 'I heard Reggie went on another tantrum today.' Later, my girl friend told me and I went to the teacher and told her off. I was suspended. I was suspended from school three times. I did everything, even steal—magazines, candy bars, stuff like that. I haven't stolen since I went into a store with my dad and stole a candy bar. He found out about it and made me go back and tell the cashier I took it. I was so ashamed I never have stolen anything again.

"My dad may not have done everything right in his life, but he saw to it that his kids did."

Reggie's dad says, "I saw to it that my kids got a college education so they wouldn't have to hustle for a buck like I did all my life. It was hard making ends meet, but I saw to it that they grew up out of the ghetto, in a nice neighborhood away from the drug addicts and the thugs. Reggie really wasn't too bad and didn't get in too much trouble. He was a little wild, like boys are, but he was a good boy. And he was a fine all-around athlete all his life."

When Reggie was seven, he started to play softball. His dad would pitch to him in the backyard. And Reggie got into games whenever he could. At nine, he started in the Little League. He was less than five feet tall and weighed less than 100 pounds. But he could throw hard and he had a big swing. He pitched some no-hitters and hit some home runs. He batted better than .500. By the time he graduated from

Little League, he was voted the Most Valuable Player.

A big league scout saw him and told him he'd make the majors some day. Reggie remembers it well: "I've never forgotten it. It was the first time I'd thought about being able to play baseball for a living."

When Reggie was in the seventh grade, starting junior high school, he still was small. He stood just an inch over five feet and weighed only a few pounds above 100. But he had athletic ability and started to play football and basketball as well as baseball. He was a hitter who liked football best of all and a jumper who did well in basketball. And he started to spurt in size. By the time he got to the ninth grade and high school he was 5'8" and 150 pounds. "Even at five-eight I could get up and stuff the ball in the basket with both hands," he recalls proudly.

He played hard and was hurt a lot. He overcame some crippling injuries. As a high school freshman, he broke his arm and missed most of the baseball season. One summer he was hit by a high, inside curve ball that didn't break and broke his jaw in five places. It had to be wired shut. "I hated it so much I pulled out some of the wires myself so I could open my mouth. A Reggie Jackson whose mouth isn't working isn't Reggie Jackson," he grins.

He was tough. He recalls, "One time I hit the line and a defensive player punched me in the mouth and broke a tooth. I asked the quarterback to call the play again and I ran right over that dude." However, another time, late in his senior season, he suffered a broken neck tackling a big back. He recalls, "I finished the game and no one even knew my neck was broken until the next day. I was in a cast for three months and the doctors weren't sure I'd walk again, much less play football again, but I was sure I would, and I did."

He averaged 18 points a game in basketball. There were games in which he averaged 10 yards a carry in football. He played defensive back as well as running back. He hit over .500 every season in baseball. He ran wild on the bases. He played the outfield and threw runners out on the bases.

By the time he graduated from Cheltenham High, Reggie was close to six feet tall and weighed 180 pounds. And the colleges were coming after him. There were fifty or so scholarship offers from such schools as Notre Dame, Michigan, Michigan State, Penn, Penn State, Temple, and others. Most wanted him to play football. "I wanted to play football," Reggie says. "I wanted to play football more than baseball. I was a heck of a football player. I loved that contact.

"But I'd had a bad experience with color in high school and I wanted to be careful what college I went to. I was invited to play for Pennsylvania in an all-star schoolboy baseball game against the finest players from Florida in my junior year. But when they found out I was black they wouldn't let me play because the game was in Fort Lauderdale, Florida, that year, and black boys weren't welcome. That was my first taste of racial prejudice, really, and I didn't like it at all.

"When I got a scholarship offer from Alabama, I knew they didn't know I was black because they didn't have any black athletes at that time. They heard or read about me and made me an offer without knowing me. I got a scholarship offer from Oklahoma and they knew I was black but made a big thing about me being the first black to play for them. They told me there would be a lot of restrictions and that turned me off.

"One of the few coaches who came to see me himself was Frank Kush of Arizona State and that turned me on. He's maybe the toughest coach in college ball, but I didn't know that then. He wanted me strictly for football, but I didn't know that then either. He knew I was good at baseball and he said I could be one of the few athletes ever allowed to play both baseball and football there. He talked about the warm weather and the long baseball schedule there. He talked about the chance to play for one of the great baseball coaches, Bobby Winkles, and on one of the great college baseball teams.

"I signed up and went to Arizona State and never regretted it. I had trouble getting to play both baseball and football, but I did get to. A football coach hassled me about dating white girls, but I was getting used to racial prejudice by then and I just went right on doing it. There weren't many black ladies in that school. I even wound up marrying a white lady I met while I was at that school.

"I liked the people there and made friends I have to this day. Gary Walker became my business partner and still is. He helped me invest some of my bonus money when I went pro and I have made a lot of money with him. When I went to Tempe I had four shirts, four pair of pants, and two pair of shoes. I didn't have an extra dime. Now I own a lot of land there.

"I fell in love with Tempe and Arizona and still consider it my second home. I spent two years in school there before I turned pro and they were two of the best years of my life," Jackson concludes.

Freshmen weren't eligible for varsity football when Reggie went there, but he played with the freshman team and scrimmaged the varsity. Running behind the blocking of Curly Culp, an enormous man who still is a star in pro ball, Reggie was effective. "Old Curly used to say, 'Follow me,' and away we'd go," Reggie recalls. But the coach, Kush, puts his players through exhausting practices and that took a lot of enthusiasm away from Reggie. "It was just too tough," he sighs.

His sophomore season, Kush converted Reggie to defensive back and that took more enthusiasm from him. "I had played defense as well as offense in high school, but I really liked running the ball best," he says. "I guess I've always been a bit of a glory guy. The running backs are the glamour guys of the game. I dreamed of making it in pro football as a running back, not a defensive back. Travis Williams, who was our running back, did make it in pro football. So did Ben Hawkins, who played defensive back alongside me. But I began to think more and more about making it in baseball."

Football coach Kush and baseball coach Bobby Winkles engaged in a tug-of-war over him. Kush said he couldn't play baseball unless he maintained at least a 2.5 grade average, which is a B-minus. Reggie maintained a 2.8, which is a straight B, and got to play baseball. He hit only two home runs as a freshman, but batted .298 and fielded brilliantly. Winkles told him that if he concentrated on baseball, he could be one of the best. He sent him to Baltimore to play in a summer league, where Reggie learned a lot and got to know his mother.

After Jackson's sophomore season as a football player, Winkles warned him that he easily could get hurt in football, not only ending his hopes of a pro career in football, but in baseball as well. That scared him some. Spring training in football came at the same time as the baseball season in the summer and Reggie went back and forth between the two until he realized he had to make a decision. "I was having a good season in baseball and I decided on baseball," he recalls. "It was quite a change of mind for me, but I had come to a fork in the road and I had to pick one path and that was that."

Winkles says, "He had a great year. He was one of the great players college baseball has had. He was getting bigger and stronger and better ever year. He could run fast and throw hard and hit the ball a mile. I could see he was going to be one of the great players big league baseball has had. I didn't know how good he was in football, but I knew how good he was in baseball. I really believed it was a better bet for him and I told him so. I don't regret it and I'm sure he never has. A lot of good athletes want to play different sports, but there comes a time they have to decide what's best for them. Baseball was best for Reggie."

"I'm sure of that now, even if I wasn't then," Reggie admits. "Bobby was one of the best influences on me I've ever had. We became great friends and remain great friends to this day. I was happy when he moved up to the majors to manage the Angels, sad when he got fired, and happy when he came to the

A's as a coach. I will be happy when he gets to manage again because he can manage with anyone. The knock on him wasn't that he wasn't a good baseball man, but that he was straight and rah-rah. He didn't like long hair and stuff like that. He might be wrong in that. But he always asked that his athletes act like men, and, at a time I was straightening myself out, he was a very positive influence on me."

Jackson matured a lot at Arizona State, both physically and mentally. At 6 feet he attained his final height and at 185 pounds he was within 15 of his big league weight. Muscles rippled through his youthful body and he was a powerful player. At Municipal Stadium in Phoenix he hit one home run 480 feet, which was farther than Willie Mays, Willie McCovey, or other big leaguers ever belted one there. He hit 15 home runs, which was a college record at that time, He drove in 65 runs in 65 games. He caught the ball and threw out runners on the bases. He stole bases.

Big-league scouts filled the stands wherever he played. General managers of several teams joined them before the last game he played. He beat out a bunt single, doubled, and hit a home run. He also made a running catch and threw out a runner with a perfect peg to home plate. "It was one of my greatest games," Reggie recalls. It was one of those games that proved how he produces under pressure. When the spotlight is turned on him, he seems to shine.

Ironically, he hoped a New York team would draft him. He thought that was his best bet for fame and fortune. The Mets had a chance to draft him, but didn't. He says, "I have since heard the Mets didn't draft me because I was black because they set a limit on the number of blacks they have on their team. I think this is true because they never have had many.

"I had gotten married while I was in college. My wife was white and I heard that turned off the Mets, too," he says. Johnny Murphy, who was the general manager of the Mets at that time, said, "It isn't true. We drafted a catcher because we needed a catcher."

Charlie Finley, who scouted and recruited the top prospects for the A's, drafted Reggie for Kansas City. "I thought that was all right," Reggie says. "I had gotten to know their scout, Bob Zuk, and liked him. The A's were a bad team, but building up, and I figured I'd get a chance to play with them. But they only offered me a $50,000 bonus to sign. Maybe that wasn't bad, but they'd given Rick Monday $100,000 to sign off our team the year before and I thought I was worth as much as him.

"I had about decided to go back to Arizona State for another year to see what would develop when Charlie got into the act. Whatever else he is, Charlie is a super salesman. That was my first taste of it. He came to me. And he turned on the charm. He even cooked breakfast for me and my father. He does things like that when he's wooing you. I ate a ton.

"He took me to Kansas City and showed me the ballpark, which was beautiful. He introduced me to Eddie Lopat, the former big league pitcher, who was his general manager. They offered me an $85,000 bonus, a new car, and whatever cash it would take for me to finish college. My father was interested in that. And I did finish.

"So I signed. That was the summer of 1966 and I had a long way to go with the A's and with Charlie Finley. Some of it was fun and some of it wasn't, but it sure was interesting," grins Reggie Jackson, who was growing up fast.

When he graduated from high school, the description of him beneath his picture in the yearbook was "Sovereign Independence." That was accurate and prophetic. It means that even then his schoolmates saw that he set himself apart from others, considered himself a leader, and was bound to do his own things in his own way.

2

The Big-Leaguer

When I first met Reggie Jackson it was his second
season in the big leagues. It was in the dressing room,
and he was putting on his uniform and admiring himself in the mirror. He said, "I love coming to the ballpark and putting on these tapered duds and going
out on that green field in a great stadium full of fans
and playing this great game." He was serious, smiling,
and full of enthusiasm.

"I want to be one of the great players. The greatest."
He had cigar boxes full of baseball cards with the

pictures of the great stars on the front and their records on the back. He sighed and said, "All those great players come and gone. You don't get much time. But they left a mark. That's what I want to do, leave a mark, make them remember I was here, make them remember me after I'm gone.

"I love baseball. I love hitting the ball hard. The sound of the bat against the ball is a sort of music. And I love seeing the ball sail high and far over the fence for a home run. I love catching the ball. The sound of the ball smacking into my mitt is music, too. And I love throwing the ball. On a line to home plate. And seeing the catcher put it on the runner sliding in and the umpire throwing his thumb in the air in an out sign.

"I love hearing the cheers of the crowd. Most people never get cheered. I get cheered. It swells me up. It makes me feel like someone. I like to see the look in the eyes of my teammates when I have done something to help them win. I like to walk into the clubhouse and see that look in their eyes, that look of respect. I want to be respected by my peers. I want to be a leader. I want to be the man. The man! This is my game and I want to be the best man in it and remembered forever."

Reggie's rise was rapid. He turned pro in 1966 and was assigned to Lewiston, Idaho, in the Northwest

League. He played only twelve games there before he was promoted.

He hit only two home runs, but both were beauties. His first was in his small home park. He hit it over a screen atop the right-field fence, and onto the roof of a house across the street from the fence. His second was in Yakima, Washington, when the temperature was below freezing and it was snowing. It was the 13th inning and Reggie's homer broke the tie and got the game over with. It not only went over the 350-foot sign in right field, but cleared a 50-foot tower beyond the sign.

"It was the longest home run I ever saw, and I saw a lot of them in twenty years as a pitcher in the big leagues," says Bill Posedel, who was scouting for the A's and suggested they promote Reggie right away. He was hitting .292 and had driven in 11 runs in his 12 games.

Jackson joined Modesto of the Class A California League. He joined players like Joe Rudi, Rollie Fingers, and Dave Duncan, who were to move up with him to the majors and become part of a championship club. Jackson hit .299 at Modesto. He hit 23 home runs, scored 50 runs, and batted in 60 in only 56 games. One of his home runs went more than 400 feet and another was estimated at almost 450 feet.

"It was exciting playing baseball for a living," he says. "The minor leagues I played in weren't much faster than the fast college league I'd been playing in. I always started slow. I got a lot of publicity as some sort of super-slugger when I got to each town and I guess I tried too hard to prove I was as good as they said I was. But I always finished fast.

"I did have an adjustment to make. Winkles was the kind of coach in college who stressed sportsmanship. I have a hot temper, but I learned to control it. I tend to use bad language, but I learned not to curse. I turned pro, and one day in Modesto I struck out and hustled back to the bench without a word. Some of the guys got on me, saying I should at least act like I cared. I saw that they cursed, threw their helmets and bats, and kicked things when they went bad. So I started to do it. It's easy to do.

"Then some of the older guys started to get on me, saying I had to learn that I couldn't hit a home run every time up and had to learn to accept the strikeouts and just try to do better the next time. They said I had to start to act professional. I didn't know who to believe. But I realized I had to believe in myself. I couldn't worry about what others thought of me. And I couldn't worry about what others thought of what I did. I just had to do what came natural.

"Sometimes I stormed and sometimes I was calm. It depended on how I felt at that time. I just had to be me. The only problem was I was just starting to find out who I was.

The Big-Leaguer

"It was lonely for me. I was meeting new people and it isn't easy for me to make new friends. I wasn't used to playing games every night and traveling from town to town, the way we did in buses. I wasn't used to living in strange towns. But I liked the playing. I wasn't making much money, but I'd gotten the big bonus, and the big money was just ahead of me."

He had been paid $500 a month to play in the low minors. He wanted $1,000 a month to play in the high minors. Charlie Finley wanted him to play in Birmingham, Alabama, in the Class AA Southern League in 1967, but offered him only $600 a month. It was Jackson's first salary argument with Finley, but not his last. It was not until the last day of spring training that they compromised at $800 a month and Reggie agreed to go to Birmingham.

"Mr. Finley called me personally and that impressed me," Reggie recalls. "Birmingham was his home town and he wanted to put a championship team in that town. He moved Duncan, Rudi, Rollie, and me to the team in that town. We had won the championship in the California League and he figured we could win the championship in the Southern League. And we did.

"Maybe I shouldn't have argued salary with the man, but I always figured I knew what I was worth. The bonus was one thing. That was to sign. The salary was another thing. That was for playing. I wanted to

31

be paid for the way I played. I knew I could play."

He could hit. He hit .293, hit 17 home runs, and drove in 58 runs in 114 games with Birmingham. He led the league with 17 triples, 232 total bases, and 84 runs scored and was voted Player of the Year in the league and all minor leagues.

He did strike out a lot, but he hit the long ball. His throwing was all right, but his fielding wasn't. He had made nine errors in about a third of the season at Modesto and he made 18, the most of any outfielder in the league, in about two thirds of a season at Birmingham.

Between Modesto and Birmingham he played at Arizona in a winter instructional league for developing pros. The A's worked on his catching in the outfield. "John McNamara was the manager and he hit me 100 fly balls a day in practice. But I didn't catch 100," Reggie smiles.

He'd make the hard catch and miss the easy one. His fielding would haunt him his entire career.

One of the reasons Reggie wanted more money to play in Birmingham was racial. He had no more than arrived in the southern city than he was greeted by bigoted remarks. He was refused service available to the white players at most restaurants in town, and in other towns around the circuit. He was turned away from apartment houses and wound up living in a black hotel. Players like Joe Rudi and Rollie Fingers had him to their apartments to dinner with their wives, but the managers threatened to evict them.

"It was a bad scene," Reggie says sadly. "I was the only black player on the team and I found out what it was like to be a black man in a bigoted town. Maybe it's not now the way it was then, but that was in the late 1960s and it should have been different there and everywhere by then.

"I felt like I deserved more money to make up for the way I had to live there. Of course, money doesn't make up for those things, but someone has to pay. I think I think less about black and white than most blacks, but there is no way a black man can make his way in a white world and not have the way he is treated leave a mark on him. I bore down and played ball the best I could, but I didn't like it there."

He played so well that at mid-season he was called to Kansas City. He tried too hard and was gone before he could get going. He was hitting less than .200 and was striking out once or twice a game when, after about 25 games, he was sent back to Birmingham. Reggie recalls, "McNamara was the manager and he told me walking back into that clubhouse would be one of the toughest things I ever had to do in my life. It was. You leave with everyone wishing you well and telling you you're going to tear up the big leagues and then you're back and the only thing that's torn up is your confidence."

Reggie sports a mustache and beard with the Oakland A's.
(Russ Reed photo)

However, Reggie returned to Kansas City at season's end, after he had led Birmingham to the championship of the Southern League and the Dixie Series playoffs against Albuquerque, the second straight title he had helped his minor league teams take. He had the opportunity to play in Kansas City with the A's before they moved to Oakland and a new team, the Royals, later moved into Kansas City. The A's moved to Oakland in 1968 and Reggie went with them as a rookie and their regular right-fielder for his first full season in the majors that year.

Reggie brought his big swing to the big leagues with him. He struck out five times in one game, matching the major league record. He led the American League with 171 strikeouts in 154 games, the second-highest total in the history of the majors to that time. He also hit a 480-foot homer against the Angels, the longest ever hit at Anaheim Stadium. And he hit two home runs against Detroit's Denny McLain in a nationally televised Saturday afternoon affair, although the pitcher went on to win his 30th game, 5–4, and become the first to win 30 in many years.

Reggie led the league's rookies with 29 home runs. He hit .250, drove in 74 runs, and scored 82. His throwing arm helped him lead the league's outfielders with 12 assists, but he made 14 errors in the field. However, his power made him one of the most promising rookies to break into the big leagues in many years.

The leagues had expanded and played as two ten-team leagues that season. The A's finished only sixth in their league, but they did win more games than they lost at 82–80 and were a coming contender with a lot of fine young players.

The following season, the leagues were divided into divisions and the A's gave Minnesota a tough time before fading and finishing nine games back in the West with an 88–74 mark. Reggie provided the power with a spectacular second full season in the big time.

That year, Jackson hit three home runs in a game against Seattle. He hit two home runs, two doubles, and a single, and drove in ten runs in a mid-June game against Boston won by the A's, 21–7. He hit two more home runs the next game at Boston. He hit two in a game at New York and the many writers in New York who had heard about him went wild over him.

"It was a thrill just playing in New York where I'd always wanted to play," Reggie remembers. "It was a thrill hitting homers in Yankee Stadium, where Babe Ruth hit so many. I walked over to the statues of Ruth and Lou Gehrig by the fence in center field and was thrilled. Reading that I was a new Ruth thrilled me. Then making the All-Star team and getting to play in the All-Star game in Washington, D.C., with all the All-Stars thrilled me."

By the mid-season classic, Reggie led the league with 37 home runs and 78 runs batted in. He not only made the All-Star team, but got more votes than any other player from the fans and got to start in it. He went hitless in it, but resumed his slugging when the regular season resumed. By the end of July Reggie had 40 home runs and was about two weeks ahead of the pace set by Babe Ruth when he hit his record 60 home runs in 1927 and Roger Maris when he topped it with 61 in 1961.

Jackson's face started to turn up on the covers of national magazines and there was a photo of him in *Sports Illustrated,* stripped to the waist, muscles rippling, which brought him a lot of teasing from his teammates. He was in tremendous demand for television, radio, and newspaper and magazine interviews and he heard and read regularly that he was the greatest new star in the game in many years. He was only twenty-four years old and it would have been surprising if he had not been spoiled by all of this.

Jenni, who was his wife then, said, "He really started to strut. He really thought he was something. Why wouldn't he, with everyone telling him he was? I understood that, but it was still tough to take. He had to have everything his own way. He came and went as he wanted. There was no talking to him. There was no living with him.

"A lot of ladies started to chase him. He'd never had anything like that and I guess it's hard to resist. I understood that, but it was tough to take. He wasn't a bad guy. Never has been. But he was spoiled by that first taste of fame and our marriage started to go bad. I guess we were too young to be married. He couldn't handle it."

Reggie admits, "I didn't handle it very well. I was carried away with my own importance. Who wouldn't be? I loved Jenni, but I loved life, too, and there was too much good going on for me in my life then for me to pay attention to her and our marriage the way I should have. Most of what went wrong with our marriage was my fault, but she should have understood better and been patient with me.

"As good as my game was going, there was a lot that was bad about it. I loved the publicity but I soon got used to it. I don't mind talking to reporters. I don't mind talking, period. But they wouldn't let me alone a minute. I'd register at hotels under my middle name, Martinez, and they'd still get to me. All they wanted to know was, was I going to break Ruth's record? How could I know? What could I say? The pressure was just terrible."

The pressure got to him. And the pitching. Opposing pitchers started to walk him, sometimes three or four times a game. They wouldn't give him a good ball to hit. He stopped hitting. He hit only seven more home runs the rest of the season. He even lost the league home-run title to Harmon Killebrew by two the last two days of the season.

Still, he wound up with a remarkable record for his second season in the big time. He wound up with a .275 batting average, 47 home runs, and 36 doubles. He had 118 runs batted in and a league-leading 123 runs scored. He again led the league in strikeouts and he was among the league leaders in outfield errors with 11, but also in assists with 14.

Reggie also led the league in slugging percentage with a .608 figure for the season. This is not a frequently listed statistic, but it may be more meaningful than the batting average. You divide times at bat into total bases, thus getting more credit for a two-base hit than a one-base hit. All hits are not equal in value. The .608 was one of the highest figures in years.

He says, "I was disappointed that I not only did not get the record with sixty or sixty-one home runs, but that I did not even hit fifty. The fact is, that was my best chance ever to do it because the pitchers did not know me or how best to pitch to me and I was young and at my strongest and swinging strictly for home runs.

"I would become a better hitter who would not go for a home run when a single would do just as well for the team, like late in a tie game with a man on second or third, but I would never again be a better home-run hitter or hit as many home runs.

"However, after my disappointment passed, I did think that it was a good year, especially for a player as young as I was. And I thought that I should be paid well for it. I was making only $20,000 a year at that time, which is very little for a big-league ballplayer, especially one who had proven himself with the sort of season I'd had.

"I was disappointed when my contract came from Mr. Finley calling for only $40,000. I asked for $60,000. He reminded me I had received an $85,000 bonus. I reminded him that was for signing, while this was for producing. He said players' salaries were raised a little at a time and I should realize I had a lot of years ahead of me to make the kind of money veterans made. I said I had earned the kind of salary I was asking for and I didn't know if I would live long enough to make big money.

"He said he had offered to double my salary and I should be satisfied with that and I was foolish if I didn't figure $40,000 was big money. Maybe he was right, but I was swollen up with my own importance at that time. He said if he gave me $60,000 after two years, what would he have to give me after ten years, $600,000? He said there was no way it would ever come to that. Well, he was wrong. The funny thing is, he hit the figure right on the head. But back in the late 1960s no one realized how much salaries would rise by the late 1970s.

"I held out and missed most of spring training before reporting late to the team and it took a lot out of me. The thing that bothered me most was I was starting to see Charlie Finley for who he was. He was a very hardheaded man who was going to give you only what he wanted to give you and would never give you what you wanted. He knew I wanted what Rick Monday got to sign, $100,000, so there was no way I was going to get it, so I had to settle for a little less. Now I wanted to triple my salary, so he only offered to double it. It turned out to be like that every time.

"He really loves the spotlight and he hated it when any of his ballplayers stole the spotlight from him. He wanted his team to win, but he wanted the credit for it. I really think he resented it when any of us had the sort of seasons that stole the spotlight."

Charles Oscar Finley was born in Birmingham, Alabama, in February of 1918. The 22nd of February, to be exact, and he took pride in the fact that he was born on George Washington's birthday. He couldn't be "the father of our country," but he wanted to be "the father of baseball." He always loved baseball and played in school and on the sand lots and became bat boy of the minor-league Birmingham team.

The son of a steelworker who was transferred to mills in Gary, Indiana, when Charlie was fifteen, he continued to play school and sand-lot baseball there, but followed his father into the mills at eighteen. He never forgot how hard he had to work for fifty cents an hour. He always reminded people that he had worked his way through night school and college.

He did work hard and developed an ulcer, which kept him out of World War II. He went to work at a war plant and worked his way up to a position of leadership. He had gotten married and had started to have children and needed more money than he was making, so he worked nights selling insurance and soon was winning awards for the most insurance sold. He always was a super salesman, a charming guy.

He was disappointed that he was not considered a big-league baseball prospect, but continued to play semi-pro ball on weekends until, at twenty-nine, he was stricken with tuberculosis. He himself had no insurance and was sad that his wife had to go to work to support their family while he was bedded down in a sanatorium. Rest is the only way to recover from TB, but his mind never rested.

During more than two years spent primarily on his back, Charles O. Finley figured out a new kind of insurance program to protect professional people who made big money and could afford to pay big premiums, such as surgeons who might lose the use of their hands. When he returned to regular life, he formed his own firm to sell such insurance. It took several years to sell it successfully, but after the American Medical Association approved it, he was on his way to wealth.

The Big-Leaguer

By the late 1950s, Finley's firm was so successful it was bringing in $40 million a year in premiums and could be operated by his employees. He preferred to operate a baseball team. If he could not play big-league baseball, he could own a big-league team. His offices in Chicago happened to be in the same building with the offices of baseball's American League. He soon was spending more time there than in his own offices.

He bid for the Chicago White Sox, the Detroit Tigers, and the new California Angels before he finally got to buy the Kansas City A's for $4 million in 1960 when he was only forty-two years old. Aside from Tom Yawkey of the Boston Red Sox, Finley was the only man who owned a team by himself, without other partners who participated in the purchase and the operation of the team. But Finley was the sort of fellow who always wanted to operate on his own.

He was welcomed in Kansas City, but soon wore out his welcome. There was a clause in the team's contract with the city that it could move to another city if attendance fell below 850,000 a season. Finley conducted ceremonies on the City Hall steps in which he appeared to burn up that part of the contract. Later, he admitted he had burned something else. He promised never to move the team. He broke a lot of promises.

He had watched Bill Veeck promote the White Sox

43

in Chicago with all sorts of special days and he copied those, but took credit for originating them. He shot off fireworks from his scoreboard, brought in pretty ball girls to chase down loose baseballs, had bat days and cap days in which he gave away bats and caps, had cow-milking contests at home plate and greased-pig-catching contests in the outfield. Others copied these, and they worked for them better than for him. They still had an old ballpark in Kansas City at the time, he usually had a ninth-place or tenth-place team at the time, and attendance was awful.

Finley outfitted his teams in green and gold uniforms because these were his wife's favorite colors. This was the first time a big-league team had gone to gaudy colors, and he and his players took a lot of kidding before others copied them. However, other ideas of his such as orange baseballs and gold home plates, which he thought could be seen better, were not taken up by the other owners. Some of his ideas, such as games between the teams of the two leagues, were good. Others, such as three balls for a walk instead of four, were not.

Finley frequently called the other owners "nincompoops" and names like that and said baseball was so far behind the times it made him sick. He made the other owners sick. Soon, he was visiting cities such as Milwaukee, Louisville, Atlanta, and Dallas, which did not have big-league teams at that time, and was talking about taking his team to those towns. The other owners, who were tired of him, asked him how much he wanted to sell his team to people who would keep it in Kansas City. He said $8 million, which was twice what he paid for it. When they got together people who would pay $8 million, Finley said he wanted $10 million.

The league gave up and let him take his team to Oakland in 1968. There was a new ballpark, but attendance turned out to be bad there too, although the team turned into a winner there. Before long, he started talking about taking his team to towns such as Washington and Denver. But whenever he set a price to sell his team, and the league got together buyers to meet his price, Charlie raised the price. The league had accepted him and now there was no way it could kick him out of its family as long as he did not break any real rules.

The rules did not limit an owner's right to run his team as he saw fit. Finley skimped on the salaries of his front-office staff and proudly pointed out that he operated with the smallest staff in the game. Sometimes he did not even have people to sell tickets, but he complained when ticket sales were slow. He complained constantly to his staff over how they did things. Soon they could see that nothing they did would satisfy him. He called them at the office all day long and at home at all hours of the night. Some of them had their home phones disconnected; Finley fired them. He hired and fired help freely.

In Kansas City and Oakland, Charlie O. had five general managers, twelve managers, and twenty-seven coaches in twelve years. He had five scouting directors and seven farm team directors in that time. He had six broadcasters and eight publicity directors. He told his general managers and his managers whom to keep and whom to trade, whom to play and whom to bench, and if they did not like it he fired them. He took the credit for winning and blamed others for losing. If his publicity people and broadcasters did not give him the credit, he let them go. Sometimes he hired people, fired them, then hired them back, then fired them again.

He did his own scouting and had a good eye for talent, and he put together a team of promising players who would become world-beaters. But he paid big bonuses to sign them, then skimped on their salaries as they developed into stars. When Reggie Jackson refused to sign for the salary offered him in 1970, Charlie O. was outraged and criticized Reggie publicly.

I was with Reggie in Arizona that spring and he said, "If Finley doesn't want to pay me what I'm worth to play in Oakland, let him trade me to New York where they'll pay me more." This was before baseball players could be free agents and make their own deals. He said, "A salesman can go to work for the store across the street, but the ballplayer can't. And it's not fair.

"The man has me in slavery," Reggie sighed.

He went to the training camps of other teams who were working out in Arizona at that time and asked some of the great black ballplayers, such as Willie Mays of the Giants and Ernie Banks of the Cubs, what they thought. They said that even if he wasn't treated fairly, he should sign and start to play because players who got late starts usually had bad years. They said he was young yet and had a lot of time to make big money and if he had a bad year he would have a bad bargaining position in other years.

When Finley compromised at $50,000, Reggie reluctantly gave in. He did report late, got off to a slow start, and had a bad year.

Shortly after Reggie struck out five times in one game the first week of the season, he was benched. From then on, he was on and off the bench. If he played poorly in games, he stayed in the lineup. If he played well, he was sent back to the bench. It was as if Finley had ordered his latest manager, John McNamara, to embarrass Reggie. The team got off to a slow start and Finley publicly blamed Reggie. Finley said Reggie still had a lot to learn and would be better off in the minors, but when Finley asked him to volunteer to return to the minors, Reggie refused. Deeply depressed, he said, "The man wanted me to volunteer to return to the minors because after the big year I had last year it would make him look bad to send me down this year. Well, there is no way I am going to the minors because I have proven I can play in the majors. If he had paid me what I was worth I would have been in camp in time to get a good start. If he will play me regularly, I can still get a good finish.

"He is a big man, but no man is big enough to break me. He can hurt me and humble me, but he cannot break my spirit.

"I have been humbled. I got too big for my britches and now I have been made to feel small. I was warmed by the spotlight but now I find it can burn the skin off your back. I do not want to have any more great years that make me ask for big money. I just want to have good years so I can get my raises a little at a time and live a good life without being hassled all the time."

It was a difficult season for him. He did not play regularly and never really got going. One night in September, after fifteen straight games on the bench, Reggie was sent up to pinch-hit with the bases loaded. Finley was in the stands that night and Reggie remembers, "I wanted to hit a home run as bad as I ever did in my life." He hit one, a grand slam, and as he came around the bases he looked up at Finley and made an obscene gesture to the owner. It was not a nice thing to do and Reggie knew it. Finley was furious, but Reggie had been too.

Later, Finley called Reggie into his office and asked the player why he had done it. Reggie replied. "Because I hate the way you treat me and the way you treat people." Finley demanded a public apology. He'd prepared a letter of apology he wanted Reggie to sign and make public. Reggie never signed it and left the office in anger. "I'll never forgive the man," he stated. Later, he demanded to be traded. "I'll never trade him," Finley vowed.

Jackson concluded the campaign with a .237 batting average, only 23 home runs, 57 runs scored, and 66 batted in. He led the league in strikeouts again with 135. He tied for the league lead with 12 errors and had only eight assists. The A's concluded their campaign with 89 victories and 73 defeats, in second place, nine games behind Minnesota for the second straight season. Finley fired the manager, McNamara, and hired Dick Williams to take over on the bench. As it turned out, Jackson and the A's had reached a turning point in their destinies.

3

Coming On

Charlie Finley had a motto he said again and again, "Sweat plus sacrifice equals success." No doubt it does, but in sports, having good athletes helps. By 1971 Finley's A's had developed into a team of good athletes.

Reggie Jackson, Joe Rudi, and Sal Bando provided power hitting. Second baseman Dick Green, shortstop Bert Campaneris, and center fielders Rick Monday or Billy North furnished fielding down the middle.

Gene Tenace and Dave Duncan were capable

catchers afield and hit with power at the plate. Duncan later was traded. Monday was traded for North. Mike Epstein hit with power and then was traded.

Some players came and went, but these were the nucleus of what turned out to be one of the classic championship teams in baseball history.

Catfish Hunter, Vida Blue, and Ken Holtzman became the key starting pitchers. Rollie Fingers and Darold Knowles were the key relief pitchers. They formed the heart of the pitching staff during the A's dynasty.

Blue was the star of the 1971 season. Although he had pitched a no-hitter late the previous season, this was his first full season. Though only twenty-two, the left-handed power pitcher was sensational.

After losing his first start, Blue won his next 10. His first 18 wins were complete games. He had won 20 games by the first week of August. For a while it looked as if he would win 30.

Blue was spotlighted the way Jackson had been a couple of years earlier. Vida was mobbed by reporters wherever he went. He found his face on the covers of national magazines. It got to him, too.

He started to lose close games, but still wound up with a 24–8 record and 301 strikeouts. He gave up less than two earned runs a game and won not only the Cy Young Award as the league's top pitcher, but the Most Valuable Player award.

Catfish Hunter, in his seventh season, broke into the 20-win circle with a 21–11 record and an earned-run average under three. Chuck Dobson won 15 games and Johnny Odom 10 despite sore arms that troubled them early in the season and sidelined them late.

Rollie Fingers started the season as a starter, but struggled and was banished to the bullpen in mid-May. There, he found his place as one of the best relief pitchers in the game. He saved 17 games and Darold Knowles saved seven.

At bat, the A's did not appear to be superstars, but they had dangerous hitters who came through when it counted. This proved to be true throughout the team's reign.

In 1971, five of the eight regulars hit around .250 or less, but all produced under pressure with timely hits. With a mere .277 batting average, Jackson actually led the regulars. He also led with 32 home runs and 87 runs scored. Bando led with 94 runs batted in, while Reggie had 80.

Five times Reggie struck out four times in a game, to tie an American League record. He struck out 161 times to lead the league for the fourth straight time to tie another league record. But he led the team with 19 game-winning hits.

After he had missed so many games the previous season, Reggie had gotten back in the groove by playing for a Puerto Rican team during the winter. He hit 20 home runs to break the Caribbean League record set by the father of Orlando Cepeda, a long-time major-leaguer who briefly played with the A's.

Veteran big-leaguer Frank Robinson managed the Puerto Rican team and the two became fast friends. Reggie says, "He taught me to control my temper, and to forget the strikeout I'd had my last time up so I could concentrate on hitting a home run my next time up. He had been hassled a lot and he taught me you have to take it and battle back."

Reggie also was surprised by a visit from the new manager of the A's, Dick Williams. "I was surprised and pleased that he would take such a long trip just to visit with me," Reggie recalls. "He promised me I would play regularly when the new season started and not to worry if I struck out or made an error. That restored some of my enthusiasm."

Reggie responded not only with clutch hits, but the fewest outfield errors, seven, and most assists, 15, he would have in his A's career.

When Reggie was being ribbed as a $50,000 bench-warmer the previous season, he kept his sense of humor by grabbing the bags of his teammates and acting as a porter at airports. They liked him for that.

"It kept me loose," Reggie remarks. "Sal Bando teased me by offering me a tip. I took it. I rooted for the team. I rooted for Rudi, my replacement. Rudi was becoming a super player. By 1971 they'd have to find room for both of us in the lineup.

"By 1971, a lot of the joy had gone out of the game

for me. Baseball had become a business to me. It wasn't just playing the game, but six or seven hours at the ballpark, seven days a week, seven months a year.

"It was not only hitting home runs and getting cheered, but striking out and getting booed. It's a lot of pressure on you from the press and the public. I had made up my mind that while I didn't want to have any bad years, I didn't want to have any great years. I just wanted to have good years, help the team, and stay out of the spotlight.

"I did get a lift in getting to play regularly. Sitting on the bench half the time the previous season really got to me mentally. But Dick Williams got me back in the lineup and left me there. He was our new manager and a good manager. He was a strong guy who stood up to Finley."

Williams did fight Finley and earned the respect of the players. From April 20th on, the A's led their division. They wound up winning 101 games, losing only 60, and leading second-place Kansas City by 16 games. With things going so well, Finley didn't want to rock the boat and largely left Williams alone.

The playoffs proved to be something else. Baltimore, which won the Eastern Division for the third straight season, was a more experienced team and would go on to sweep the best-of-five pennant playoff series from the Western winners for the third straight time.

Coming On

Blue took a 3–1 lead into the seventh inning of the first game at Baltimore, but a four-run rally finished off the young pitcher and his side, 5–3. Hunter was hit for four home runs in the second game and Mike Cuellar stopped the A's, 5–1.

With others of his starters sidelined with sore-arms, Williams had to turn to Diego Segui for the third game back in Oakland and he was no match for Jim Palmer and the Orioles, who won 5–3, before a disappointing crowd of fewer than 35,000 fans.

It seemed as if it was over before it started and the A's were stunned. Jackson, who'd had a good series with a .333 batting average on four hits in 12 times at bat, including two home runs, nevertheless seemed the most stunned.

He sagged onto the dugout steps in disappointment at the final out and lay there a long time with his head in his arms and without moving. The others all left until he was the last one left in the dugout. Finally, slowly, he pulled himself together and made the long, slow walk up the steps to the dressing room.

There, in that quiet room full of disappointed players, Reggie sat on his stool in front of his locker with his head down. He was asked how he felt. He said, "I feel like we had our chance and let it get away. It's very hard to win a pennant. I guess we just weren't ready but I don't know if we'll get other chances."

They would.

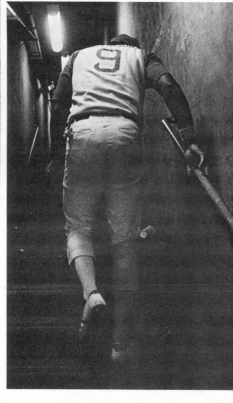

Deeply disappointed following the A's playoff loss in 1971, Jackson sits slumped on the dugout steps before beginning slow, sad climb to the clubhouse.   *(Oakland A's photos)*

Coming On

They fought all the way to win it all in 1972.

Spring training opened without Vida Blue. After his sensational season Blue and his manager, Bob Gerst, asked for $100,000. Finley had signed Hunter for $50,000, with the promise that he would not pay another pitcher more. Finley offered Blue $45,000. Blue called a press conference to announce he was going to work for a firm that sold toilet seats, instead.

The season started with the A's without Blue. Finley offered and Blue finally accepted a contract calling for $50,000 in salary and $13,000 in side monies, but Finley wanted to announce it as $50,000 and Blue as $63,00 and they were apart awhile longer before Blue gave in.

However, he did not report until May and wound up with a 6–10 record. While he would bounce back, Blue never again would be as overpowering a pitcher as he had been. Finley took a lot out of Vida as he had taken out of Reggie earlier. Reggie had warned Vida the holdout might hurt him, but Blue didn't believe it.

Hunter topped the staff with a 21–7 record and allowed only a little over two runs a game. Ken Holtzman, who came with North in the trade for Monday, took up the slack with a 19–11 record. "Blue Moon" Odom had a 15–6 record. Fingers won 11 games and saved 21.

Jackson had a good, not great, season. He hit .265 with 25 home runs. He scored 72 runs and drove in

75. He struck out 125 times, but for the first time since he had been in the league, he did not lead the league in strikeouts. George Scott of Milwaukee struck out 130 times.

Epstein led the team in home runs with 26 and Bando led in runs batted in with 77. Rudi tied Reggie for second with 75. Rudi and Duncan hit 19 home runs each. Duncan slumped at season's end and Tenace took over as catcher and turned out to be the home run hero of the World Series.

Campaneris led the league in stolen bases with 52.

The A's also led the league in mustaches. Reggie reported with one and Williams talked Finley into letting the player keep it. To rib Reggie, relief pitchers Rollie Fingers, Darold Knowles, and Bob Locker also grew mustaches.

Finley was fascinated and announced that a Father's Day game would be "Mustache Day" and every fan who showed up with a mustache that day would be admitted free and every player who had grown one would get a bonus of $300.

Holtzman said, "For three hundred dollars I'd grow hair on my feet."

Every player on the team grew a mustache. But a bitter Blue shaved his off before the game on the big day and was the only one who did not get a bonus. However, mustaches became the team trademark and they were nicknamed "the Mustache Gang."

Many went on to grow beards, Reggie included. The A's were the first team since the early days of baseball to play with beards and mustaches and they set a trend that was copied by many men in sports.

This was the first season Finley outfitted them in fancy uniforms to set another trend that was copied by many teams. The players had so many possible combinations of green, gold, and white shirts, pants, socks, and shoes that they had to check a posted daily announcement to see what they would wear each game. They were a colorful, fighting bunch.

As a team, the A's had fights off the field among themselves more times than could be counted and on the field twice with other teams. Finley found the fights funny and nicknamed his team "the Fighting A's."

Finley was in fine form all season. He made 65 different moves with 41 different players. He traded, bought, sold, released, and picked up players all season long. Eleven different players played second base, including catchers and outfielders. It was Finley's idea to pinch-hit every time one of his light-hitting second basemen was due to hit.

Somehow, Williams maintained order on his team. The White Sox got off to a fast start, but the A's took over first place the end of May. By the middle of July, they were eight games in front. Less than one month later, the A's had slumped and fallen out of first place. There were rumors that Williams would be fired.

Finley never was going to do what was expected. He promptly signed Williams to a new three-year contract. By the end of August, the A's had regained the lead. They won 14 of their last 20 games to finish with a 93–62 record and fight off the White Sox by 5½ games to win a second straight divisional laurel.

Despite this, the A's drew less than one million fans at home for the second straight season. A team must draw more than a million fans to be considered respectable. Actually, a team must draw 1½ million fans or more to make money, on the average. Finley was having fun, but losing money.

Post-season games are expected to be sellouts, but the A's seldom sold out their 50,000-seat ballpark. They had the first two playoff games at home in 1972, but the first drew less than 30,000 fans and the second only slightly more than 30,000. The A's had a cold ballpark and cool fans. A number of fans were faithful and frenzied, but the city did not support the team respectably.

Nor were the San Francisco fans in Oakland's sister city across the Bay supporting their team, the Giants. The A's were playing well, if the Giants were not. The northern California bay area, a beautiful, if foggy and chilly area, was not exactly hot territory for baseball.

Once again, Finley started to talk about taking

his team elsewhere. He also wondered whether it wouldn't be wise for the Giants to move if the A's didn't. He felt that the area could support only one team. He probably was right. But the talk persisted for years with neither team taking off for a new territory.

In 1972, the A's might not have developed strong support in their area, but they were on the verge of becoming one of the best teams in baseball history.

They took on Billy Martin's Detroit Tigers in the playoff. The A's were hungry to erase memories of their having been swept out in three straight games by Baltimore the year before. This series was to go five games, the first to go more than three games in the four years since these divisional playoffs to decide the league pennants had begun.

The A's entered the playoffs with reliever Knowles sidelined with an ailing arm. Early in the playoffs they lost shortstop Campaneris when he was suspended for throwing his bat at a pitcher. Hunter started the first game, but Fingers was the winner by the time the team had come from behind in the last of the 14th inning to win, 3–2. Odom pitched the second game and shut out the Tigers on three hits, 5–0. Campaneris had three hits, stole two bases, and scored two runs. In the seventh inning, Martin may have ordered his pitcher, Lerin LeGrow, to "brush back" Campy. The pitch hit Campy in the ankle and the player hurled his bat over the head of the pitcher. Martin, who was well known for ordering brushback pitches, charged Campy and had to be restrained from fighting him.

After the A's arrived in Detroit to resume the series, American League president Joe Cronin announced that Campaneris had been suspended for the rest of the playoffs. Finley was furious and even went to Cronin's hotel room to complain.

The Tigers prolonged the series by winning the third game from Hunter, 3–0, as Joe Coleman struck out 14 A's. Then the Tigers tied the series by winning the fourth game, 4–3 in 10 innings.

The A's appeared to have won the pennant by taking a two-run lead in the first of the 10th, but Detroit rallied with three runs in the home half on a wild variety of hits, walks, wild pitches, and errors.

However, the A's seemed to do best when they got themselves in one kind of trouble or another, and they won the fifth and final game, 2–1.

Jackson, who had five hits in the series, walked and scored the first run, but pulled a hamstring muscle in his leg sliding home and colliding with the catcher. Tenace, who had only the one hit in 17 times at bat in the series, singled in the second, decisive run.

Odom started, but complained he had trouble breathing in the sixth inning, and Blue came in to finish up. The two pitched superbly, but Blue was bitter that he had not gotten to start a game in the series. In the dressing-room celebration later, he taunted Odom for "choking up" and asking out of the game. Blue Moon went at Blue and the two exchanged blows before being broken apart. By then, this sort of foolishness was expected among the A's.

Propped up on crutches, Reggie was smiling while he watched the celebration. But there were tears in his eyes. He had been told his injury was severe and he would not be able to play in the World Series. Something he had long looked forward to had been taken away from him by his own hard play.

Having won the first pennant since they were a Philadelphia team in 1931, the A's went into their first World Series in 41 years. They faced the Cincinnati Reds, who had topped Pittsburgh's Pirates in another five-game playoff for the National League pennant.

The Reds had put together the powerhouse array of catcher Johnny Bench, first baseman Tony Perez, second baseman Joe Morgan, and outfielder Pete Rose, which would form the nucleus of the club which would dominate the decade in the National League.

The A's went in as the underdog. They were without slugger Jackson and reliever Knowles, although shortstop Campaneris was restored to eligibility. However, they had dangerous hitters and superior pitching with which to confront the Reds.

The Series opened before sellout crowds of more

than 50,000 fans in Cincinnati's Riverfront Stadium. Wearing green and gold outfits, waving pennants, smiling broadly for the television cameras, Finley sat with family and friends in a box seat by the dugout and all but stole the show.

However, it was the players who came through in the clutch. Nine of 12 games in the playoffs and World Series were decided by one run and the A's won six of them.

Gene Tenace became the first player ever to hit home runs his first two times at bat in a World Series. He drove in all the runs as the A's won the opener, 3–2, behind Holtzman, Fingers, and Blue. Joe Rudi hit a home run and saved the game with a leaping catch against the fence in the ninth inning as the A's won the second game, 2–1, behind Hunter and Fingers.

At the airport, 8,000 fans waited for the team. Finley told broadcaster Jim Woods to see that the players stayed together to be greeted by the fans. However, on arrival, several slipped away. Finley shouted at and shoved the broadcaster, and later reprimanded the entire team in a temperamental tirade.

Nevertheless, close to 50,000 fans attended each of the A's games at their Coliseum, one of Oakland's better shows of support for the team.

In the third game, Campaneris made a mistake in the field for the only run as Jack Billingham blanked the A's and beat Blue Moon and Blue, 1–0. The A's rallied to win the fourth game in the ninth inning, 3–2, behind Holtzman, Blue, and Fingers. Tenace hit his third home run.

One loss away from defeat, the Reds won the fifth game, 5–4, as Rose opened the contest with a home run on the first pitch from Catfish Hunter and closed it by singling in the winning run in the ninth off reliever Fingers. Tenace hit his fourth homer of the series, a three-run home run, but it was wasted. Only Babe Ruth, Lou Gehrig, and a few others ever had hit as many in a World Series.

Back in Cincinnati, the Reds won the sixth game to even the series at three victories apiece and send it to a seventh and final game. Blue was behind by only 2–1 when Williams relieved him. Vida stormed off angrily. When the Reds ran the score to 8–1 off the A's relievers, Vida threw things in the dressing room.

Bad plays and bad hops in the field helped the A's to a 3–2 win in the seventh and decisive game. Tenace doubled in the winning run and was voted MVP of the Series. He'd hit .225 with five home runs and 32 runs batted in in 82 games during the season, but he hit .348 with four home runs and nine runs batted in in seven games of the Series.

Blue Moon started the seventh game, but got help from starters Hunter and Holtzman and reliever Fingers before the final out sent the A's into a wild celebration in the dressing room.

Finley mounted the podium on which the heroes were being interviewed and stood with his arms outstretched, receiving cheers. Someone said, "Good God, he's going to proclaim himself king."

The A's were to reign awhile.

In 1972, Reggie Jackson said, "Watching my team win the World Series without me was strange. I wanted the A's to win, but I wanted to help them win. To be truthful, I wanted to win it for them. I felt left out. I felt terrible. I couldn't sleep. I couldn't eat. I was never as nervous when I was playing. I hated not playing. When my teammates won, I was happy for them, but sad for me. When you're part of a team you want to be part of its victories.

"A team that can win two titles in a row is some-

(Top) Joyous celebration after final out as A's win seventh and final game of 1972 World Series from Cincinnati for first championship. That's Campy Campaneris, top center, manager Dick Williams with uplifted No. 1 finger, and Vida Blue behind him. *(Ron Riesterer photo)*

(Bottom) Sal Bando, left, and Catfish Hunter carry winning trophy from 1972 World Series victory over Cincinnati through Oakland Airport. *(Russ Reed photo)*

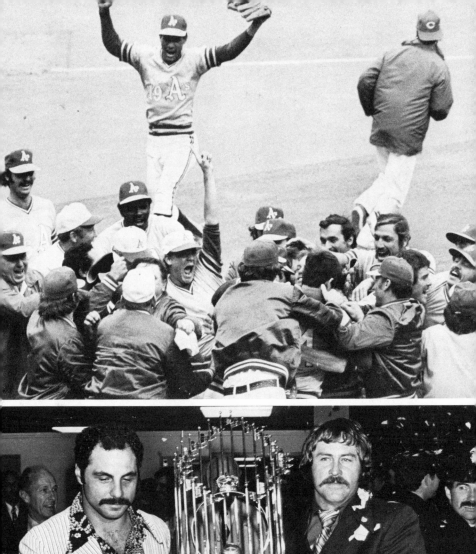
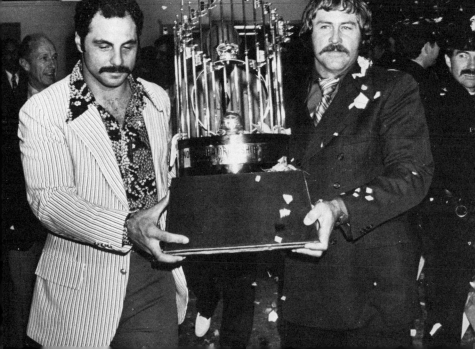

thing else, an outstanding team. I determined to do my best to help my team win its second straight championship. I decided I had to bear down every day to use my ability in the best way I could. I realized I was cheating myself, my family, my friends, my fans, and my God if I didn't."

4

The Champion

A newly determined Reggie Jackson became the driving force behind The Angry A's in 1973.

He averaged .293 and led the league with 32 home runs, 99 runs scored, and 117 runs batted in. He also led with a .531 slugging percentage. He struck out 111 times, but others struck out more. He made only nine errors afield.

He missed two weeks near the end of the season with another pulled hamstring muscle, but his season was sensational.

Reggie not only was voted Player of the Year in the Major Leagues by *The Sporting News,* but received all 24 first-place votes to become a rare unanimous selection as Most Valuable Player in the American League.

"I feel like I have finally fulfilled my God-determined destiny," he pointed out proudly.

He had a lot of help, of course. Bando hit 29 home runs and drove in 98 runs. Tenace took over at first base and hit 24 home runs and drove in 84 runs. Deron Johnson contributed 19 home runs and 81 runs batted in after Finley acquired him. Hunter, Holtzman, and Blue all were 20-game winners. Fingers saved 22 games.

The season did not go smoothly, of course. A's seasons did not go smoothly.

Finley hired and fired front office people and bought, sold, and traded players all season long. When the team got off to a slow start, he started to criticize Williams. Even Reggie criticized Williams and his coaches. He called them "too critical." But when Jackson criticized Williams and the coaches, Finley defended them and gave them new contracts.

As player representative, Jackson fought with Finley all season, defending his teammates. Although not all the A's liked the outspoken, temperamental player, Reggie had become the team leader and he took pride in his performances for the team on and off the field. He liked being a leader and admitted, "This season has been more fun for me than any other."

At twenty-seven, he was at his playing peak. In his sixth full season, he had the maturity to deal with the reporters without taking too much out of himself. He really enjoyed the camaraderie of the clubhouse and joined joyfully in the constant kidding with which this tough team kept itself loose.

The White Sox spurted to an early lead in the division, but were finished when slugger Richie Allen broke his leg late in July. The A's took over first place on that same night. They slipped out of the lead for a while while Hunter was sidelined with a broken finger, but regained the lead for good in mid-August and pulled away to win by six games over Kansas City with a 94–68 record.

Finley had put out a promotional film of the previous season's success. He titled it, "Finley's Heroes." Each player got a print and they marveled at the many scenes of Finley cheering in the stands. However, he suffered a slight heart attack late in the 1973 season. But when the playoffs started, there he was, wheeled about in a wheelchair, watched over by his personal heart specialist.

One minute he was being wheeled into a hotel, huddled in a blanket, looking as if the end were near; the next minute he was out of his chair and doing stunts with a group of pretty cheerleaders in the lobby.

The first two games in Baltimore attracted crowds of between 40,000 and 50,000 fans. Baltimore knocked out Blue in the first inning of the first game and went on to win, 6–0, behind Jim Palmer's pitching. The A's bounced back to beat the Orioles in the second game, 6–3, supporting Hunter with four home runs.

The teams went to Oakland with the third game scheduled for a holiday, Columbus Day. The A's had drawn more than a million fans for the first time in Oakland and had an advance sale of more than 30,000 for the game. However, when it rained, American League president Joe Cronin postponed the game.

Finley thought that Cronin had not waited long enough to see if the rain might stop. He was angry and raged at the president in an argument at the stadium.

The game was played before more than 30,000 fans the next day, but that was far less than a full house. The A's won it, 2–1, on the three-hit pitching of Holtzman and the second home run of the series by Campaneris in the 11th inning.

Fewer than 30,000 fans turned out for the fourth game. The A's appeared to have the series won with a 4–0 lead behind Blue's two-hit pitching going into the seventh inning, but Baltimore rallied to tie the game in that inning and won it on Bobby Grich's home run in the 11th. For the second time in three seasons, Blue had been beaten by a Baltimore seventh-inning playoff rally.

After the game, Fingers said something about Blue's pitching which Blue Moon Odom thought unfair. Blue Moon jumped at Fingers and the two wrestled before being broken up. In the curious way of the A's, one player fought another in defense of a player he, himself, had fought only a year earlier in the same sort of situation.

Jackson was asked whether the incident might upset the team. "No way," he said. "No blood was spilled. Nobody worries about anyone else's feelings on this team, anyway. Nobody is afraid to say what he thinks on this team. We fight among ourselves, but we get together to fight as a team against other teams."

The turnout for the fifth and final game was fewer than 25,000 fans, smallest in the five-year history of the playoffs, but the A's went on to win their second consecutive American League pennant easily, 6–0 behind the clutch pitching of Catfish Hunter.

Jackson had a poor playoff with only three hits, but what was not generally known was that he was playing under the pressure of a death threat to him delivered to the team and relayed to Reggie by Finley. It came in a letter threatening Reggie with death if he played in the playoffs and World Series.

It was signed by "The Weathermen," a militant group which had been connected to killings in the past.

The FBI provided him protection and Reggie also called on a friend, Tony Del Rio, a massive man who stood 6′ 5″ and weighed 290 pounds, to be his bodyguard.

Reggie admitted he had been nervous, but determined to put it out of his head, as he went into the World Series. "I've waited a long time to finally get in a World Series and I want to help my team win," he vowed.

He would. But not without turmoil.

In Reggie's rookie year, he jammed his thumb. Before the following game, the A's team physician, Dr. Harry Walker, announced there was no way Reggie could play for a few days. However, when the game began, Reggie was playing. When the writers reached Walker, he told them the injury wasn't as bad as he'd believed.

It was learned later that Finley had spoken to the doctor and decided Reggie was fit, after all. When Reggie found out, he was so angry he took a scalpel from the doctor's bag and cut the bandage off his thumb so savagely he sliced open the thumb.

When Gene Tenace was shifted to first base, Finley said Dr. Walker had been treating the player for a shoulder so sore he could not throw well and so could not catch well. Tenace said he had not been treated for a sore shoulder. Dr. Walker would only say, "That's Charlie's business and I'm not going to get involved in it." The players started to call Finley "the medicine man."

After the A's beat the Mets, 2–1, in the first game of the World Series before fewer than 45,000 fans in Oakland, they lost a sloppy second game, 10–7, in 12 innings before almost 50,000 fans. Jackson had four hits, but the New Yorkers won with the help of two errors by reserve second baseman Mike Andrews in the last inning.

Prior to the Series, injuries had reduced the A's roster to 24 players. Finley tried to get an infielder, Manny Trillo, added at the last minute, but by the rules it was too late and he was refused. Finley had the fact that he had been refused announced to the crowd at the start of the Series. Cronin hinted that he would fine Finley.

Without Trillo, the A's turned to Andrews. After the errors, Andrews and Dr. Walker signed a statement prepared by Finley that the doctor had been treating the player for a shoulder injury and the player was unable to play any more.

Andrews was sent home and Finley sent a copy of the statement to Cronin, again requesting that Trillo be added to the roster as a replacement.

When the players found out about the incident, on the flight to New York, they were furious. When they met in New York they threatened to refuse to play without Andrews. They played, but wearing black arm bands in protest. They felt that Andrews had been embarrassed unfairly. "All players make errors," remarked Reggie.

He telephoned Andrews and was told by Mike that there was nothing wrong with his shoulder and he had signed the statement only on the threat that he would be blackballed from baseball if he didn't.

When Williams heard this, he called the team together and told them this was one thing too many to take. He would not work for Finley any more and would resign as manager after the Series.

When baseball commissioner Bowie Kuhn heard the details he reprimanded Finley for being "an embarrassment to baseball," ordered Andrews reinstated, and refused the request to add Trillo to the roster. Andrews did rejoin the team, but many of the players on the team told Finley they wanted to be traded away from him and his team.

Despite turmoil like this, the A's were the type of team that could put everything else aside, go out and play ball, and produce under pressure. The A's went out and won the third game, 3–2, on a run-scoring single by Campaneris in the 11th inning. In the clubhouse Odom hollered, "Dissension does it again!"

However, the Mets won the fourth game, 6–1, to tie the Series at two victories each the next night.

The Champion

The game was marked by the reappearance of Andrews, who received a standing ovation from the enemy fans. Jackson said, "It sent a shiver down my back." Williams had been ordered by Finley not to play Andrews, but the manager pinch-hit him anyway. He grounded out, and did not play again.

The Mets won the fifth game, 2–0, as Jon Matlack and Tug McGraw combined to frustrate Blue, who pitched the top pressure game of his career and still lost. At that point the Mets had taken the lead in the Series, and as the two teams flew back to Oakland the A's were within one loss of losing the Series.

Except for his four hits in the second game, Jackson had been having a disappointing Series with only one other hit. Reggie said, "We've had our backs to the wall before and battled back. We will again." Rudi said, "Reggie's our leader and he will lead us." Some called Reggie by the nickname "Buck." Tenace said, "Buck will break it open."

Before the sixth game, Tenace stopped by Jackson's locker and said, "Buck, big guy, they've got Tom Seaver pitching, but we're counting on you." Seaver was the best pitcher in the other league, but Reggie really responded to such challenges. He said later it was his greatest thrill. He doubled in runs in the first and third innings. Those were all the runs Seaver allowed, but they were enough to beat him.

Reggie singled and scored the final run in the ninth and the A's won, 3–1, behind Hunter and the bull-pen to tie the Series and send it to another seventh and final game.

Sellout crowds of close to 50,000 fans supported the A's in the sixth and seventh games.

They were roaring as the seventh game began with Holtzman hurling against Matlack. They really roared as little Campaneris hit his third home run of post-season play in the third inning, a two-run home run, to put the A's in front. After Rudi singled, Jackson hit a home run deep into the right center-field stands to make it 4–0.

The Mets never caught up. They rallied, but Reggie made two spectacular catches in the outfield to stall them, and Fingers, making his sixth appearance of the Series, and Knowles, making his seventh, pitched great relief.

A woman ran onto the field and ripped Reggie's glove right off his hand even before the final out. When it ended, 5–2, and the fans stormed onto the field, Reggie's burly bodyguard escorted him off safely.

There was little celebration in the A's dressing room. The players said Finley's treatment of their teammate Andrews had taken all the joy out of it for them. Jackson said, "We're just businessmen making a buck. We have a job to do and we go out and do it. It's no longer a game for us. I blame Finley for this

The A's parade in vintage cars through downtown Oakland following 1973 triumph in World Series with New York Mets, the second of three for Reggie Jackson's crew.

(Ron Riesterer photo)

and for the loss of Williams, the best manager in baseball."

At the victory party the A's staged at an Oakland restaurant that night, Reggie and Blue Moon had to be pulled apart after they got into an argument.

Reggie had been voted Most Valuable Player in the Series to go with his MVP award for the regular season. He had come through when it counted and he was proud of his performance. "I always wanted to be the kind of person you could depend on when the money was on the table," he said.

Now, he wanted big money—more than $100,000.

"A hundred grand is symbolic of the top players in sports," he said. "I'll get a hundred grand as sure as the sun is going to come up tomorrow. It's sure. I want more. I am at the top of my profession now and I expect to be paid accordingly. The man owes me money he wouldn't pay me in the past. He'll pay."

He did, though he didn't want to. He offered $85,000. Reggie asked for $135,000. When the two sides couldn't get together, new rules called for an impartial arbitrator to decide. Jackson took his case to court. The arbiter heard both sides and decided Reggie was worth what he wanted.

Some A's and other players won and some lost in arbitration, but Reggie received the largest award of all.

The Champion

Finley wasn't too happy. He took his unhappiness out on Williams. Originally, he had wished his manager well in any new job he took. However, when Williams signed to manage the Yankees, Finley announced Dick still had a year to go on his contract with the A's and would be held to it unless the Yankees gave him either Thurman Munson or Bobby Murcer, their best ballplayers. The Yankees refused. The league, which had fined Finley for his acts at other times, sided with him this time.

Jackson said, "What can you expect from Finley?" Williams said, "I'm disappointed and I won't work for him again." Dick decided to sit out the season

Despite triumph, it is a depressed manager Dick Williams and wife who listen as Charles O. Finley tells them how he did it on victory stand following manager's resignation.

(Russ Reed photo)

until his contract expired. However, later in the season Finley let him go to the Angels as manager, asking and getting a good deal of money for him. Finley, who had hired and fired Alvin Dark as his manager in Kansas City, rehired him to manage his A's in Oakland in 1974.

Dark had been fired as manager of the Giants for having made remarks which suggested that blacks and Latins were lazy and didn't play the game as hard as whites. He denied that he had such feelings, but the blacks and Latins looked at him with suspicion when he took over the team. At one point, he told Reggie he was not yet returning Bando to the lineup after an injury because Bando was white and, "Just between you and me, we all know black boys heal faster than white boys."

Reggie was stunned. He said nothing at the time. Later, he said, "I don't think he even knew what he was saying. If he did, he wouldn't say it to me, a black. He was raised in the South with certain attitudes and I guess they stay with you whether you mean for them to or not."

Others were less considerate. Dark had been away from baseball a few years and it took time for him to catch up to the changes in the game. After he had mismanaged one game, Bando stormed into the dressing room complaining, "That man couldn't manage a blankety-blank meat market." Sadly, Dark happened to be walking right behind him. They talked it out, but the incident made headlines, as did everything and anything the A's did.

Finley tore into Dark a few times, too. One time he burst into the manager's room and tore into Dark so loudly that everyone in the clubhouse could hear him: "I don't know what the blank you're in this game for, but I'm in it to win. And if you don't get your blanking rear in gear, you're gone. We won two straight titles without you, and we can win a third without you."

While Dark had divorced his wife of more than twenty years to marry a pretty young stewardess, he had become a deeply religious man who described himself as a "born-again Christian who believes in the Bible and practices its teachings." He quoted scripture in his talks to his team, and at first the players ridiculed him for it behind his back.

However, in time they came to see that he was sincere and, if not perfect, he was patient. He took criticism and the turmoil on the team in stride. And there always was turmoil on the team, of course. The most serious incident in 1974 involved Jackson and Billy North.

Jackson and North had become buddies, but early in the season Reggie bawled out Billy for not running out a ground ball. Billy was a player who sometimes got down and lost interest when he was not doing well, while Reggie was a player who took his role as a leader seriously.

"What business is it of yours?" North asked angrily. "Who are you? I've seen you not run balls out." Which was so true it made Reggie even madder. He said it was the whole team's business and all the players suffered when one player didn't put out. Billy said that Reggie was only a player and when he was a manager he could criticize other players. He stormed off and for a while he wouldn't speak to Reggie.

When he started to speak, Reggie wished he'd stop. Billy rode Reggie regularly, making one wise-crack after another. Reggie tried to take it in stride, but it began to bother him and he started to talk back. The two bickered constantly.

One day Reggie took a telephone call that was meant for Billy. It was a girl who was dating Billy, but used to date Reggie. The girl asked Reggie about his problems with Billy and they talked awhile. When Billy found out about it later, he raged that Reggie was trying to take his girl friend from him.

Reggie ran at him and wrestled him to the ground. Others pulled them apart. But Billy cursed Reggie and Reggie went at him and wrestled him to the ground again before others pulled them apart again. The two wrestling matches weren't much, but Reggie suffered a sore shoulder and one of the peace-makers, catcher Ray Fosse, suffered a wrenched neck that bothered him from then on.

Naturally, the incident hit the headlines and Finley flew into town to talk to the two. To Reggie's surprise he did not ask anyone what had happened, but blamed Reggie, saying he'd been a troublemaker from the time he joined the team.

Reggie took it, but it took a lot out of him. After thinking it over a few days, he telephoned Finley and told him, "You do not have to like me, but you do have to treat me like a man." He concluded by saying that the true troublemaker on the team was Finley himself, and hung up on the startled owner.

It turned out to be the sort of season Reggie had not wanted to endure again. Late in the season, *Sport* magazine asked him to pose as General George Patton and do an interview with George C. Scott, who had played Patton in a prominent movie. The picture was supposed to make Jackson look like the leader of the A's, which he was. But he was afraid it would make him look foolish, and it did. Murray Olderman wrote an accompanying story that ridiculed him for posing as Patton. Later, Reggie criticized Olderman before a post-season game and was himself criticized for doing this.

There were other incidents during the season. Reggie said, "There may have been more turmoil on our team than on others, but all teams have troubles. The season is long, the schedule hard, and the players get tired.

"The pressure is on an athlete all the time and if

he isn't going good, he is going to be touchy. Some players are more sensitive than others. I'm sensitive to criticism and don't take it too well. It took me a long time to learn to roll with the blows. I tend to say what I think and it took me a long time to learn not to be so outspoken. I've had my share of hassles with the other players and my managers and I have to accept my share of the blame.

"I really want to be liked, but I think it's unrealistic to expect every player to like every other player on a team of 10 or 20 or 25 players and there are bound to be differences. Since we had won anyway, I think we didn't try as hard to get along off the field as most teams do and took a kind of funny pride in our ability to fight off the field and win on it.

"We did take pride in our ability to perform and produce under pressure. And in a strange sort of way, all our differences with Finley and with one another off the field served to unite us on the field. The world didn't think we could go on the way we had and go on winning, so we were doubly determined to do what everyone thought we couldn't do."

Hunter won 25 games, his fourth straight season of 20 or more. He allowed only 2½ earned runs a game, lowest in the league. He won the Cy Young Award as the top pitcher in the league. Holtzman won 19 games and Blue 17. Fingers won nine, saved 18, and led the league with 76 appearances as a pitcher.

The Champion

Although his statistics slipped when he suffered his sore shoulder and he missed the last two weeks of the season with a sore leg, Jackson wound up with a .289 batting average, 29 home runs, 90 runs scored, and 93 driven in. Less than the season before, it still was respectable.

He struck out 106 times, made 10 errors, had eight assists.

Tenace hit 26 home runs, Bando and Rudi 22 each. Bando drove in 103 runs and Rudi 99. North led the league with 54 stolen bases. Campaneris had 34, Herb Washington 29, and Reggie 25. Washington was Finley's latest innovation, a pinch-running specialist.

Reggie always could run and steal bases, but suffered from pulled muscles too frequently to run and steal regularly. Green and Campaneris were the centerpieces of a splendid defense. As the season wore on, Dark seemed to get back his feel for the game and began to make all the right moves. "We came to respect him as a good baseball man and a Christian gentleman," Reggie remarks.

Texas, then managed by Billy Martin, finished five games back. After the A's clinched the division title, they didn't celebrate. So The Angry A's stormed to their fourth straight divisional laurel and were on their way to a third straight American League pennant.

The Orioles arrived in Oakland with 28 victories in their last 34 games. They had won nine straight games to end the season as the league's eastern champion for the fifth time in six seasons. They made it ten straight as they hit three home runs off Hunter to win the opener, 6–3.

The A's had slipped back below 1 million in attendance during the season, in fact below 850,000, and only a little more than 40,000 turned out for the opening playoff games, but the fans cheered as the A's squared the series in the second game, 5–0 behind Holtzman's pitching and home-run hitting by Bando and Fosse.

The Orioles' winning streak was snapped. This was a strong team with superb pitching which might have had a dynasty had Oakland not taken it away from them.

Oakland took command in the third game as Bando hit a home run for the only run of the game. Blue with a two-hitter outpitched Palmer with a four-hitter for Vida's first triumph in four post-season starts.

The A's captured the series in the fourth game as Jackson's double drove in the winning run in a 2–1 game. It was the only hit of the game for Oakland, but the A's took advantage of nine walks by Mike Cuellar and two by Ross Grimsley, one coming before Reggie's big blow.

The A's were 12th and last among the 12 teams in the American League in hits through the season, but only two teams scored more runs. The A's got their hits when they needed runs, and they got the runs they needed to win. Their pitching protected slim leads.

In the playoff finale of 1974, Fingers relieved Hunter and saved the victory after the Orioles had one run in and two runners on in the last of the ninth. As usual, the A's had what it took to win the thrilling games.

So, it was on to the World Series against the Dodgers. And on the eve of the classic in Los Angeles, Blue Moon Odom needled Fingers about his problems with his wife and the two came to blows. Others broke it up, but Fosse fled to safety in the showers.

Odom said, "It was just a fuss between friends. But we're ready to play ball now." Fingers said, "This is our way to get ready for a big game."

In the first game, Jackson hit a home run in the first inning to get his team going toward a 3–2 victory. Fingers saved the victory for Hunter.

The second game was something else. The Dodgers took a 3–0 lead off Blue into the ninth with Don Sutton pitching. After Bando was hit by a pitch, Jackson came through by doubling him to third. Rudi then drove both in with a single and it was 3–2. But Herb Washington pinch-ran and got picked off first for a big out as the rally fell short.

Some criticized Washington, but Reggie refused

to. "The man hasn't played a lot of ball and, anyway, it happens to all of us," he said. "We'll get 'em in Oakland."

Fingers helped out Hunter and with the help of two sensational fielding plays at second base by Dick Green the A's held off the Dodgers to win the third game, 3–2. Afterward, Bill Buckner of the Dodgers labeled the A's "lucky" and said only Jackson, Rudi, and Bando could play for the Dodgers. It was a sort of silliness and only served to stir up the A's.

Fingers helped out Holtzman and with the help of another sensational fielding play at second by Green to end the game, the A's won the fourth game, 5–2. Holtzman hit a home run himself, and Jackson got a key hit and scored a key run with a marvelous slide home, hooking away from the catcher's tag.

Before the fifth game, Finley asked Jackson to accept the victory trophy from Bowie Kuhn in ceremonies in the dressing room after the game and douse his bitter rival with champagne. Reggie thought it would be fun. "If we win," he said.

"You'll win," Finley said.

They did.

Blue and Sutton hooked up in a 2–2 tie until the seventh. Oakland fans filled left field with garbage aimed at Buckner and delayed the game. The temperamental Mike Marshall, who was pitching relief, refused to warm up during the delay. When the game was resumed he tried to throw a fastball past Joe Rudi and Rudi ripped it for a home run and a 3–2 lead.

Reggie remarked, "Marshall is good, but thinks he's better than he is. You have to be warm, you have to be ready for a Rudi. You can't take the top players lightly. Rudi knew Marshall was going to try to blow one by him and he was ready. Rudi is always ready."

Fingers relieved in his fifth straight game. He got in trouble in the eighth but got out of it when Buckner tried to stretch a single into a triple when his hit took a bad bounce past North and he was thrown out on a relay throw by Jackson, who backed up North on the play.

"It was my business to back up Billy," Reggie recalls. "Instinctively I saw what Buckner was up to as I got the ball. I knew what he was thinking. He was human and he wanted to be a hero.

"I was saying to myself, 'Hey, man, where you going? Hey, man, don't try this on me. Hesitate. Wave at me. Holler, "Hey, Jack." Let me know you know I'm there. Don't pass go. Don't collect no money.'"

Jackson threw to Green who relayed the ball to Bando for the big out. The A's took the money game, 3–2. Reggie, who had six hits in the Series, caught the last out on a fly ball off Fingers, who was voted MVP of the Series.

Encouraged by Finley, Reggie playfully doused

startled baseball commissioner Kuhn with champagne in a hilarious moment on national TV.

The A's had won a third straight World Series championship. They had proven themselves a great team. Jackson had proven himself a great player, a clutch player, and a leader.

He says, "We had done something few teams in history had ever done, but we went through a lot to do it. I was proud of my performances and my team, but it took a lot out of me and out of us. I had a funny feeling we had just about reached the end of the road and I wondered what my life would be like from then on."

He was right about the A's and Finley nearing the end of their dynasty. And at the age of 28, with seven seasons in the big leagues behind him, Reggie had reached a turn in the road.

5

The Player
and the Person

Reggie Jackson stands a little over 6 feet in height and weighs between 200 and 210 pounds from year to year. He is as big as most heavyweight boxers and has 17-inch biceps, which are bigger than most heavyweight champions have had. He also has heavily muscled legs, bigger than those of the biggest boxers.

"My strength is in my strength," he says. "I have great strength in my legs and especially in my hands and arms. I use my strength. I take the big swing and hit the long ball. I can swing at a ball which appears to be past me and hit it hard enough to hit it out of the playing field to the wrong field. When I hit a ball just right I hit it as far as anyone."

His two longest home runs probably were one he hit off a sign in right field 517 feet from the plate in Minnesota's Metropolitan Stadium in 1969 and one he hit off a light tower in the upper deck of the right-center-field stands 520 feet from the plate in Detroit's Tiger Stadium in the 1971 All-Star Game. Since the latter hit the tower on the rise, it might have traveled more than 600 feet had it not been stopped.

The Detroit blow brought every player on both benches and most of the fans in the stands to their feet and the announcers and writers said it might have been the hardest-hit ball of all time. Dock Ellis of Pittsburgh was the pitcher and he said, "I almost take pride in it. No one could hit it harder or farther." It is still remembered with awe.

"When you hit one like that, everyone is in awe," Jackson says. "It gives the hitter a tremendous sense of power. You know no one can hit a ball harder or farther. You feel like the heavyweight champion must feel. You have beaten the best. You have scored a knockout. You are the best. You are the heavyweight champion of baseball. Maybe I have more ego than many, but anyone would feel proud. Most won't talk about it.

"All us big guys love the long 'taters," says Reggie, using a word invented by George Scott to describe home runs. It is a shortening of the word potatoes. No one knows why Scott chose to use the word, they only know players like Reggie love to use such colorful terms. "When you hit the long 'taters, you are king of the hill," says Reggie.

"When you swing like I do, you are going to strike out, too, like I do. I am supposed to hit home runs, so I go for them. Other players are supposed to get on base to be driven in, and I am one of the players who is supposed to drive them in. I do. I hit 30 or so home runs every year and drive in around 100 runs every year. I also strike out around 100 times every year.

"They talk about the home runs Babe Ruth and Mickey Mantle hit, they don't talk about the fact they set records for strikeouts, too. I expect to hit a lot of home runs so I expect to strike out a lot, too. It used to make me mad, but now I see that's how it has to be. It doesn't bother me, except when I strike out with a man on second or third and us a run behind late in a game. That's when it's time for me to just get the bat on the ball and hit in somewhere to move the men around and maybe get them home.

"I am a good enough hitter now to get my bat on the ball any time it's anywhere near me, and there are times when that's all I should be thinking of and not getting selfish and going for the long one. A lot of people criticize me because I'm not a .300 hitter. Well, I could hit .300 in a season if I wanted. I could hit

.325 or more, if I went for the hits and not the home runs. It would cut my home runs in half. It would be wasting myself.

"I always wanted to be a complete player, like Willie Mays, who was my idol. Willie hit singles and home runs. He ran the bases with the best. He caught the ball and threw it better than anyone. It took time for me to see I'll never be the player he was. I can run bases with the best. I can steal with anyone. My percentage of successful steals is one of the best. But when I start to pull off steals, I start to pull muscles. My legs can't take it. So I've learned to lay off except when it's needed.

"I have bad legs, a bad back, and bad eyesight, but I can still play ball.

"I can throw with anyone. And I can catch the ball. But I seem to lose my concentration at times when I'm in the field. But I rarely lose my concentration at bat. I don't care if it's snowing or raining, I can concentrate.

"I love the challenge. It's very hard to hit a hard-thrown baseball, you know. The best don't hit it for hits four times out of ten. Most don't hit it for hits three times out of ten. A brain surgeon wouldn't succeed with that sort of percentage. Or a lawyer. Or a basketball player. But that's baseball.

"It's one-on-one. Two-on-one, really. The pitcher and the catcher against the batter. They've built a

book on you and they're trying to figure out what to
throw you that will beat you. I'm trying to figure out
what they're gonna throw me. I don't guess. I anti-
cipate. I'm looking for certain pitches, but if I don't
get 'em I adjust to what I get.

"I don't care if they take their time to talk it over,
if the pitcher walks around and rubs up the ball trying to make me upset, I'm ready. I like it low, but I
can hit it high. I like it inside, but I can put it out
from outside. I am bearing down on every ball that is
thrown me. I don't want to die, but brushbacks don't
bother me. I won't let 'em.

"The toughest pitcher I have to hit against is Nolan
Ryan because he throws the hardest and he throws
at you. He tries to scare you. He scares me. I admit it.
But I make myself stand in there to take my swings
against him. One time when there was nothing at
stake, I told the catcher to tell him to throw me one
right down the middle, his strength against mine. He
did and I hit it 450 feet to the deepest part of the
park and it was caught. Returning to the dugout, I
patted him on the butt. It was fun.

"It's fun for me, hitting. And the more there is at
stake, the more it means to me. There are times when
I am maybe hurting or just not hitting well. All hitters
have slumps. I don't know why. You get out of rhythm.
Your timing goes bad. You're just not swinging good.
The ball looks like a marble and the bat feels like a

light pole. It's the only time I lose my concentration. Because slumps bother me. But when it's a big game, I always seem to get going.

"I really respond to pressure. I really love it. I usually start to swing good. The ball looks as big as a grapefruit, the bat feels like a magic wand. I have complete concentration. I bear down. The big games bring out the best in me. Maybe because I've come through so much. It gives me confidence. Some players don't want the ball in the clutch. They're afraid of making a mistake, of looking bad, of letting the team down. I want the bat. I feel like I'll hit the ball.

"The only thing better than the long ball is the big hit in the big game. It can be a home run or a single. The big thing is to come through in the clutch, to produce under pressure, to win. I learned how to win from a manager like Dick Williams, a pitcher like Catfish Hunter, a batter like Sal Bando. You have pride. You're a professional.

"This is how I make my money. I make a lot of money, but it is not easy money. I don't feel any sympathy for the owner. If he wasn't making it, he wouldn't be paying it. The top players who come through when it counts are the ones who draw the two to three million fans a season. We are in the entertainment business and I entertain. It is a fact that because I am colorful and get in controversy I can earn more than a George Foster, who is a better hitter, but has not had the chance to come through as I have and does not attract crowds as I do.

"There was a time I thought a hundred grand a year would be unbelievable. Times have changed. Now, what's $500,000 a year when a Robert Redford makes a million dollars a movie, when a rock star gets a hundred grand a concert? We're paid for the people we pull in. I understand that the fan resents it. The average Joe may not make in his lifetime what I make in a year. He never hears the cheers. But when I hit a home run in a World Series, I hear his cheers. He boos me for the money I make, but cheers me for the home runs I hit.

"A lot of people ask a lot of me. I give till I've got no more to give and they get on me when I stop giving. I'm emotional. I ride a roller coaster of emotions. Some days I'm glad, some days I'm sad. It's the way I am and I can't change. I've learned to take a lot in stride, but there's always a lot going on inside.

"My life is not what I thought it would be. The game is not what I thought it would be. I've done more and won more than I dreamed of, but a lot of my life has been a nightmare. I've made more money and had less happiness than I would have thought possible. It's made me aware of my Maker. I have gotten a lot of religion. I think God has given me a lot, so I try to give something back. I think God has taken from me because he wants to keep me humble. I may not always act like it or sound like it, but I have a humble side. I think God has gotten me through some hard times and I thank Him for helping me by trying to help my family and friends."

Reggie's father, Martinez Jackson, remains a tailor: "Jack the Tailor." His shop is in a poor part of downtown Philadelphia. He makes about $20,000 a year. He says, "Reggie helps me with anything I need and the only time I asked for money to purchase some property he gave it to me. I tell him, you give me the money and I'll retire, but the truth is I'm not ready to retire. I'm only sixty or so and I've been a tailor forty years. I get a lot of business because my boy is who he is. People come in to talk baseball. You have to remind him who he really is sometimes, but he's been a good boy and I'm proud of him."

Reggie bought a home for his mother, Clara, in Baltimore and furnished it for her. He has given to his sisters and brothers although some of them have done well for themselves. Joe is a career man in the Army. Jim is a graduate of Boston University and a practicing attorney. Jim's wife, Maria, received a doctorate from Harvard. Beverly's husband owns a furniture store. Dolores was married, but divorced. Reggie lavishes gifts on his brothers' and sisters' children. He gave sister Tina the car he was awarded as MVP of the World Series.

Reggie married the former Jenni Campos in 1968,

separated from her in 1971, and was divorced from her in 1973. She has said, "He's a good guy and there's a lot to him, but he wasn't ready for marriage and he didn't work at it. He got carried away by his success. Someday he may settle down and make a marvelous husband, but I got to him too soon." He says, "She's a wonderful woman and I admit that our marriage not working was mostly my fault, but she might have been more patient with me and given me time to get my act together. I was spoiled by my success, but I think a lot of fellows would have been. I was never a bad guy to her."

He adds, "She read good books, while I read comic books. I'm kidding, but you get the idea—she made me feel dumb at times. I come from a broken home and I never knew a good marriage. I thought all the head of the house was supposed to do was go out and earn a buck and put food on the table. I didn't know how to cater to a wife. I've matured now and I can stand up to anyone now. I'm gun-shy so I've steered clear of another marriage so far, but I date only ladies I could marry. Someday I will marry one. More than anything, I want to have a house full of kids. I really love kids."

For a long time Reggie carried a torch for Jenni and used to telephone her to talk over his troubles with her and would go to her whenever she had troubles, but they've drifted apart now. He does not date a lot of women friends, but he dates a few women friends a lot. They are really nice and he treats them nicely. He is black and many of them are white. Jenni was a Mexican-American. He has been criticized for this. He says, "There are 200 million people in this country and 180 million of them are white. If I restricted my girl friends and my friends to blacks I would be leaving out a lot of people. I do not believe in discrimination of any kind."

His best friend is Gary Walker, whom he met while at Arizona State. An insurance man and a brilliant businessman, Walker formed United Development in Arizona with Jackson; they deal in land development. They own not only raw land, but shopping centers and apartment complexes. They have bid for ball clubs in various sports and Reggie someday may be the first player-owner of a team. Walker has made Reggie a millionaire many times over and Reggie says of Gary, "I trust him with my life." Gary says, "We have a wonderful relationship. If I have helped him, he has helped me more."

Reggie says of friendship, "When you leave your friends, they should feel better for having been with you, as I feel better for having been with them. Whether you have given each other ten cents or ten minutes, you leave something with the other person. You can't have many real friends, because you only have so much of yourself to give and you have to be willing to give whatever you have to a friend."

He gives a lot to his friends. He gives a lot to many

people. For many years he has had a youth foundation in Arizona which gives financial and moral support to black, Indian, Mexican-American, and white kids, primarily troubled youngsters. He gives financial and moral support to youth causes in northern California and New York. When he signed with Standard Brands for a candy bar, "Reggie," he set up his earnings from it in a trust fund to provide scholarships for needy youngsters.

He can afford it, of course, but he does it without seeking credit from it or publicity for it.

Reggie has a manager, Matt Merola, an attorney, and others who help him conduct his complex business affairs. He has pieces of partnerships in car dealerships with Ed Dohnt in the San Francisco-Oakland Bay Area, a fellow who befriended him early on and annually gave him new cars to use for free. Reggie buys a lot of cars, ranging from new sports cars to vintage Fords, from Rolls-Royces to Volkswagens.

He is well paid for television commercials he does for Volkswagen and others. He has been maybe the best of the athletes when serving as the baseball expert for telecasts of big games in which he was not playing, and was especially effective hosting a sports celebrity television show in which he had to interview other stars. The producer soured on him because he was not available for the shooting as often as he should have been and because he insisted on doing the interviews in his own way, but admitted that Reggie was the most effective host the series has had. Reggie is quick and bright, speaks well and speaks frankly, and makes an impressive appearance on such shows.

There are a lot of ballplayers who are bad interviews, either because they do not want to talk or cannot talk well. Many resent the time it takes and the loss of their privacy. Reggie always has taken time for the press and has surrendered a lot of his privacy to reporters. He enjoys the spotlight, of course, and loves being "center stage." He talks frankly and talks well. He is honest with his opinions. This has hurt him at times. Other players have resented what he has said about them. But he has said worse things about himself when he was down on himself.

He has been burned by the spotlight at times. When he was holding out that first time in Oakland, a reporter told him he was in the right, to stick to it, to fight Finley to the finish—and then turned around and wrote newspaper pieces ripping into Reggie as being in the wrong and hurting the team by not giving in to Finley and refusing to report to the team.

Such incidents have hurt Reggie's image with the public and although few are as free with their fans as Reggie, he has been hassled by the public constantly. In New York, a young tough hassled him outside the ballpark and insulted a member of his family. Angrily, Reggie chased the kid through the parking lot. He never caught him, but when the boy fell he charged Reggie with knocking him down and sued.

The Player and the Person

Another time, when a lady asked Reggie for an autograph while a movie was playing in a darkened theater and Reggie put her off, she cursed his date, sued him, and he counter-sued. It is simply not easy to lead a normal life as a celebrity in the spotlight wherever he goes.

In New York, Reggie has been burned by criticisms of his salary, his relationships with Thurman Munson and other players, and his arguments with manager Billy Martin. Reggie has been right at times and wrong at times, but has been made to bear the brunt of the blame for all the internal troubles on the team. He probably was right in most of his arguments with Martin, a fiery fellow who cannot get along with others, a manager who has won wherever he has managed, but been fired wherever he has been. Reggie probably was wrong in his situation with Munson, saying in an interview shortly after he reported to the team that he would be the leader Munson had not been with the Yankees.

Reggie always wants to be the leader, as he was with the A's, but he had earned it with that team and he should have waited to earn it with the Yankees. Reggie formed close friendships on the A's, such as one with Joe Rudi, but he does not make friends easily and he did not give himself a chance to make friends on the Yankees, who resented his being regarded as their "savior" when he arrived. "I feel alone and lonely on this team," he sighed sadly.

He is sensitive to others as well as to himself. He has a wisdom which helps him see both sides of a problem. To give one example, there was a time when "Campy" Campaneris was in trouble with his teammates because he was missing too many big games with too many injuries they considered imaginary. Reggie told me, "Campy is a stranger in a strange country. He knows nothing but baseball and when he can't play any more he'll have nothing to do and nowhere to go and no way to feed his family. He puts himself ahead of the team out of fear for his future. I don't like it, but I understand it."

Few players would have.

Leonard Koppett, the veteran writer for the New York *Times* and *The Sporting News,* says, "Reggie is the best reporter among the athletes." By that he means that Reggie, more than other athletes, sees where the best story is in a situation and gives it to those who are interviewing him, rather than giving them the meaningless, careful comments others do. He still does this, despite having been burned. He is one of the few players who remain available to reporters in the worst of times, whether after hard defeats or controversial incidents. He just chooses his words more carefully now than he once did and does not respond as angrily to criticism.

He spends a lot of time with a few friends outside of baseball and he spends a lot of time alone listening to soul music. He spends a lot of time tending to house plants at his various "homes." He had a house he called home in Arizona and in season has an apartment on fancy Fifth Avenue in New York, but now calls the condominium he has in the Oakland hills home. It cost him $85,000 when he bought it some years back, but it's worth two or three times that now. When it burned down one year, he simply had it built back up. He could afford it, but he lost a lot of personal treasures.

One of his most treasured possessions has been a painting of Jonathan Livingston Seagull, the bird who became a hero through a book and a movie. Reggie says, "He wanted to be free to do something others had never done. He was a lot like me."

Reggie is a prisoner of his importance and he cannot move freely about towns without being hassled. He seems more comfortable in a diner like "Lois The Pie Queen's Place," where he is accepted as a friend, than in the fanciest restaurants, where he is welcomed as a celebrity. He spends a lot of time tinkering with and polishing his collection of cars and a lot of time at Tony Del Rio's shop, where cars get expert care. Reggie also spends a lot of time driving his cars very fast over roads that carry him away from wherever he was. He sometimes gets speeding tickets, but it is an "escape" for him.

We were on our way to Lois The Pie Queen's Place

for breakfast one morning and Reggie was speeding his sports car at close to 100 miles per hour on highways, side roads, and city streets, startling the drivers we darted past, stealing looks at me to see how I was taking it.

"Scaring you?" he asked, grinning.

As I had ridden with race drivers such as Richard Petty and Parnelli Jones, speeding was not one of the things which scared me. Told this, he seemed disappointed. He gunned the sleek car even harder. The grin faded for a while, then returned.

"Well, when I die, it probably will be at the wheel of a car, crashing into a tree," he announced triumphantly.

A death wish? Reggie speeds through life recklessly. He says and does things impulsively, no matter how much he regrets them later. But I think that more than anything else he is driven by a desire to be the best at anything he does.

He is a good enough driver to race. He is a good enough ballplayer to make the Hall of Fame. He may not, because he has been controversial. If not, he will be disappointed. But he now expects to be disappointed. Life has been a disappointment to him. He would be the best husband, father, friend, the best person anyone could be if he could, but life has been full of frustrations for him. Still, he has triumphed over many obstacles.

6

Man on the Move

One of the great teams in the history of baseball, Charles O. Finley's Oakland A's came to a turning point in their destiny after winning their third straight world championship in 1974.

Catfish Hunter had signed a two-year contract before the season started. It called for a salary of $100,000 a year, but half was to be paid into a special pension plan which would provide him money for twenty years after he retired.

When Finley's lawyers told him the money paid

into such a plan could not be deducted from his income taxes the way straight salaries paid players could be, he did not put the money into the plan.

When Hunter learned that the payments were not arriving at the insurance company which was to operate the plan for him, he told his lawyer, who told him Finley had failed to live up to the contract and so Catfish could be free of Finley.

Up until that time, baseball players almost always remained the property of the teams that held their contracts even if the teams had to make adjustments on their contracts.

Finley was prepared to pay Hunter the money owed him, but never figured he would lose his property.

However, Hunter took Finley to court and the judge not only ruled that Finley had to pay the player the $50,000 owed him, but declared that the contract had been broken and the player was a free agent.

This and similar court decisions at that time shook up organized baseball. The ruling meant that players could not be considered property, like pieces of land, and could not be forever owned by baseball teams to be bought, traded, and sold as management wished.

Baseball leaders had to draw up new rules so that veteran players could be free when their contracts were broken or ran out and could make the best deals for themselves with new teams, without their old being repaid except in draft choices.

110

This was a threat to the competitive balance in baseball. The richest teams could offer the sort of money which would bring them the best players. But it gave the players the sort of freedom other people in other jobs have. For instance, a salesman or a mechanic or a teacher can take another job in the same profession if offered more money or better working conditions or a nicer place to live, so why not an athlete? All sports leagues have had to draw up similar rules.

Hunter received offers from other teams over the winter, and early in 1975 signed a five-year contract to pitch for the New York Yankees for a reported $3.2 million. This amounted to more than $600,000 a year, but was to be paid him over twenty years.

Soon many other players, including Reggie Jackson and other A's, would take advantage of their new freedom to make good deals for themselves with new teams. With teams bidding against one another for the best players, salaries went two to four times higher. Suddenly, players were being paid the sort of salaries that used to go only to leading entertainers.

Before being forced to offer freedom to players, baseball leaders had tried to compromise by offering arbitration on contract disputes. If owners and players could not agree on new terms, the owner made an offer, the player said what he wanted, and an arbitrator decided which side was more in the right.

Before the 1974 season, many players went to arbitration with the owners over their contracts. Nine A's, the most of any team in the majors, went to arbitration with Finley. Five won. Jackson won the biggest raise of any players in the majors. He won a $60,000 raise.

He had been playing for $75,000 a season. Finley offered a $10,000 raise. Reggie asked for $135,000. The arbitrator ruled in favor of Reggie, ruling in effect that he had been underpaid for years. So had been many of the A's.

Finley was in financial trouble. His insurance business was having its troubles. The Internal Revenue Service was suing him for back taxes. His wife was suing him for divorce and asking for alimony money. His baseball team was not drawing well or making much money.

Finley sold a basketball team and a hockey team he also owned, but refused to sell his baseball team. He cut his front office staff to fewer people than usual, even though he already had the smallest staff in the majors. He cut the meal money paid players while living on the road. He tried to hold down the size of their contracts, but lost.

After his A's won their third straight Series in 1974, he offered few raises. This time, nine who had new contracts to sign took him to court, but only two won. Reggie, who was seeking another raise to $168,500, had to settle for $140,000. He was the only loser who had been offered a raise by Finley and his was only $5,000.

Despite their success as a team, most of the players determined to flee Finley as fast as possible. With the opening of the free agent market, most decided to seek better deals as soon as their contracts expired. Reggie, for one, was determined not to sign another contract with Charlie.

The loss of Hunter hurt them. Jackson said, "Finley is supposed to be a smart businessman, but letting go of Catfish is dumb baseball business. With this team I think we could have gone on winning championships, but it is going to be hard without him. Soon, a lot will be leaving and this team will win no more titles."

He was right.

The A's still had enough left in 1975 to win their fifth straight Western Division title in the American League by seven games over Kansas City with a 98–64 record.

Blue won 22 games, Holtzman 18, and Fingers won 10 and saved 24. Reggie averaged only .253, but tied for the league lead with 36 home runs, scored 91 runs, and drove in 104. Tenace hit 29 home runs, Billy Williams 23, and Rudi 21. Tenace, Williams, Rudi, Bando, and Claudell Washington each drove in 75 runs or more.

Reggie struck out 133 times, but provided the

power that pushed the A's to the top again. There really was no race as the Royals were not yet ready to mount a real challenge. The Texas team fell apart as Billy Martin was fired at mid-season, later in the season taking over the Yankees.

However, the pennant playoffs were something else. Whether it was the lack of Catfish Hunter to lead off or a loss of spirit is hard to say, but by a spirited Boston team, winning its first pennant since 1967, the A's were swept in three straight games.

The A's still had pressure-pitcher Holtzman to hurl the opener in Boston, but four errors did not help his efforts and the Red Sox romped to a 7–1 victory behind the three-hit pitching of Luis Tiant.

Jackson hit a two-run home run to help the A's to a 3–0 lead early in the second game at Fenway Park, but Boston batted out Blue in the fourth inning and with the help of home runs by Carl Yastrzemski and Rico Petrocelli rallied to win, 6–3.

After a day's rest, the best-of-five series resumed before almost 50,000 fans in Oakland. Dark turned back to Holtzman, but with only two days' rest the veteran was knocked out and the A's were beaten, 5–3.

Reggie ripped two hits and drove in a run in the finale and had four hits and three runs batted in during the three games, but he had little help. Bando had six hits and drove in two runs. No one else produced.

So, the dynasty was done; the A's string of three straight American League pennants and World Series championships was snapped. They still had their run of five consecutive divisional titles, but that would end the following year.

Ironically, the A's set an attendance record at Oakland with 1,075,518 in 1975, but as the team was torn apart support for it would fade fast.

Speaking at the Redwood Chapel Community Church, Dark said of Finley, "If he doesn't accept Jesus Christ as his personal savior, he's going to hell." It wasn't clear where Charlie was going, but after hearing of this Charlie told Alvin to go on his way and named a new manager, Chuck Tanner.

Finley found himself at the trading deadline in 1976 with seven unsigned stars. He signed Blue, but traded Reggie and Holtzman to Baltimore for Don Baylor, Mike Torrez, and Paul Mitchell, and sold Blue to New York for $1.5 million and Rudi and Fingers to Boston for $1 million each.

Commissioner Kuhn vetoed the sales, saying they were "'bad for baseball." His reasoning was that the rich teams should not be permitted to purchase players without an exchange of players of comparable value. Finley felt this unfair because the players were playing out the last years of their contract and he would lose them to the new free agent market without any compensation at all. But when he took his case to court he lost.

And he did lose his players. Jackson would follow Hunter to New York in 1977. Torrez and Holtzman would follow. Baylor and Rudi would go to the Angels, Bando to Milwaukee, Campaneris to Texas, and Fingers and Tenace to San Diego. A lot of players made a lot of good deals for themselves and made the moves their newly won freedom allowed them, but no team was torn apart as was Charlie O's Angry A's.

The A's slipped into second place in 1976 as their attendance dropped off a quarter of a million fans. After losing most of their remaining stars, they fell into last place, 25 games below .500 and 38½ games out of first place in 1977. Finley went through two more managers and after the season sent Blue to San Francisco, completing the destruction of a championship club.

When Jackson was traded to Baltimore on the second day of April, 1976, it shook him up. He had asked to be traded many times, yet Finley had refused so many times that Reggie really didn't think it would happen. At that time, when he was playing out the last year of his contract, Reggie really expected to make the move the following year on his own.

There was so much turmoil on the team the early part of the 1976 season with stars being told they had been sold, then, after packing up and reporting to their new teams, being told the deals had been voided and having to pack up and report back to their old Oakland team, that everyone was depressed.

"Catfish had gone, now I was going, and I knew the others were going. It had been such a great team and now it was not a team any more. We all wanted to get away from Finley, but we had been through so much together and had won so much together it was a shame we couldn't go together. It was like a family breaking up. It was like leaving a family. I wept," the emotional Jackson admitted.

"I didn't want to report to Baltimore. I didn't want to play for the Orioles. I wanted to pick my own team and my own place to play. I knew I could do that at season's end, but I still had to get through this season. I thought of sitting out the season, but I wanted to play. They wanted to renegotiate my contract, but I didn't want to. I wanted to negotiate with other teams too. They couldn't accept that.

"I sat at home awhile trying to figure out what to do. I finally decided to report and play out the season with the Orioles, but I was a month late, I had missed a lot of games, and it took me another month to get into shape and get sharp. Naturally, the team wasn't too happy with me. Management and manager Earl Weaver treated me well, but, even though I was close to my mother and sisters in Baltimore, I wasn't too happy either. Still, I did my best."

In an effort to keep him, the Orioles gave him a

$60,000 raise which brought his salary for the season to $200,000, but he still refused to sign a new contract for the following season. The raise made several, like Holtzman, unhappy, and the Orioles wound up trading him to New York, but the Yankees used him little that season and the following season and his career headed downhill.

The Orioles had a top team. Jim Palmer, who was to win his third Cy Young Award in four seasons, and Wayne Garland were top pitchers. Mark Belanger and Bobby Grich were an outstanding double-play combination. And Lee May and Jackson provided power. Jackson was named to the American League All-Star team for the fourth time. He averaged .277, hit 27 home runs, scored 84 runs, and drove in 91 runs in only 134 games.

Jackson did strike out 108 times to tie the old American League record with a ninth straight year of 100 or more strikeouts. He also led the league with 11 outfield errors to tie the league record with five different years leading in this unfortunate category.

Jackson showed considerable courage during the campaign. He was hit in the head with a pitch and damage was done to his right eye. The doctors at first feared he would lose his sight in the eye, but it healed and he was out only a week. However, he admitted that it frightened him.

He said, "I think the brushback pitch is the worst

part of baseball. It is not fair to try to make a man afraid. A hard-thrown ball can kill a man. I was hit by a baseball as a boy and my jaw was broken in several places. This time I thought a ball might have blinded me. When I came back, I was afraid of being afraid.

"I went out to the park early with Jim Frey, one of our coaches, to take batting practice. I told him to throw at me. I wanted to make sure I'd be able to go up there and swing when the game started. You have to grit your teeth and stand up there and take your swing. If pitchers feel you're afraid, they'll throw at you from then on."

The first pitch thrown to him in the game, he hit for a home run. The next time he was thrown at, by Clay Carroll of the Chicago White Sox, he went down, got up, and went after the pitcher. There was a near riot, but Reggie was restrained by six of his teammates. Afterwards he said, "If they throw at me, I'm going to go after them. But after it's done, it's done. I don't carry grudges around with me."

At one point in the season, Reggie tied an American League record by hitting home runs in six straight games. He also led the league in slugging percentage for the third time with a .502 percentage, having led with .531 in 1973 and .608 in 1971.

His hitting helped keep the Orioles in the race for a while, but Billy Martin's New York Yankees pulled away to win their first pennant in twelve years by

10½ games over the runner-up Orioles during the regular season, and by three victories to two in the playoffs with Kansas City, before being swept out of the World Series in four straight losses to Cincinnati.

Less than two months after the season ended, Reggie Jackson was a Yankee. He was the most publicized star available in the free-agent market. Ten teams made big-money bids for him. Montreal and San Diego offered him more money than the Yankees

Reggie tries on his new cap on reporting to the Yankees for the first time at training camp at Fort Lauderdale, Florida, in 1977. *(Author's collection)*

did. Montreal offered him $4 million for five years. San Diego offered $3.5 million for five. The Yankee offer, after many negotiations, came to $2.93 million for five years. But Reggie wanted to play with a contender, which the Yankees were and the others were not.

The Yankee offer amounted to an average of $600,000 a season, but was to be paid out over twenty years, providing him protection for his future. It included an additional $1 million interest-free loan he could use to invest, but would have to repay later.

He thought he might be happier at home in California. Everyone in baseball admires the Dodgers as an outstanding organization, which treats its players well. Reggie thought he'd like it in Los Angeles. When he got the final offer from the Yankees, he called the Dodgers and asked if they would match it. A more conservative club, not at that time active in the free-agent market, they would not. Little did they know that less than a year later he would haunt them.

So Reggie signed with the Yankees and appeared for the announcement at the Americana Hotel in New York on November 29, 1976, wearing a gray flannel suit with gold buttons and a vest, a gold watch and gold championship ring, looking every inch the prosperous businessman he had become and standing in front of the TV spotlights with a broad smile on his face and a Yankee cap perched on his head.

He had always wanted to play in New York. He felt his star had been hidden in Oakland. He once said, "If I played in New York, they'd name a candy bar after me." He thought that the Baby Ruth bar had been named for Babe Ruth. He did not know it was named for the baby, Ruth, born to Grover Cleveland while he was President of the United States.

Nevertheless, Standard Brands soon signed Reggie to a contract calling for a new candy bar, "Reggie," to be developed and introduced within one year, long before Reggie's World Series home run heroics. The money was to go to youngsters, including a block of seats bought for them for every Yankee home game. "I am in the Big Apple, where I belong," remarked Reggie.

"There is not enough money in the whole world to cover this hot dog," laughed Darold Knowles when asked about his former teammate. Reggie's reputation as a player who likes the way he plays remained larger than of that person who might pop off, but had a habit of backing up every boast. "I guarantee you no team I play for will ever be swept out of a World Series," he boasted on the day he signed with the Yankees.

He would back that up, too. George Steinbrenner, the owner of the Yankees, seemed to sense this. He said, "I have bought not only a colorful performer who can pull in paying fans, but a player who produces under pressure." The Yankees, who became known as "the best team money can buy," had become contenders for the first time in many years and Steinbrenner had determined to provide the help the team needed to become world champions once again.

The Yankees had been by far the most successful franchise in sports. They had won 30 pennants and 20 World Series championships. With Hall of Famers like Lou Gehrig, Babe Ruth, Bill Dickey, Joe Di-Maggio, Mickey Mantle, and Yogi Berra, they won five World Series in a row at one point, four in a row at another, and dominated the game until the middle 1960s, when they finally slipped.

They were at a low ebb when Steinbrenner bought the team in January of 1973 for $15 million.

Steinbrenner was born on the Fourth of July, 1930, into a family that had made a fortune in shipbuilding and shipping on the Great Lakes out of Ohio. He learned the business, bought out his father, and made the firm more successful than it had been before. He increased his personal fortune tremendously. An ardent athlete as a young man, he burst into big league baseball by buying the Yankees.

Steinbrenner was indicted for having made under-cover contributions to the campaign to re-elect Richard Nixon in 1972. Presumably, by not disclosing a $25,000 contribution he could have been covering up an attempt to buy business favors from the administration. He pleaded guilty and escaped with $35,000 in fines, but was barred from baseball for 1½ years by Commissioner Bowie Kuhn for "conduct detrimental to baseball."

He was not forced to sell his team and apparently still operated it from behind the scenes. When he was reinstated, he stepped back into the spotlight with renewed determination to restore the Yankees to glory. He loved the spotlight and spoke publicly and frequently of how he would spend what he had to spend and do what he had to do to make his team the best team in baseball.

George Steinbrenner was not unlike Charlie Finley in many ways—a man of enormous energy and enthusiasm who believed in running his businesses in his own way. "It may not be the only way, but it's my way, and as long as I own something, I will operate it my way," he said. He spent money more freely than Finley, but was as fast to hire and fire, wheel and deal as Charlie.

Steinbrenner told his managers how to manage. Billy Martin was a manager who did not like being told how to manage. But Steinbrenner hired Martin midway in the 1976 season because Billy was a winner. He had won wherever he went, but lost his jobs everywhere. He was temperamental and constantly in trouble. Martin was hard to handle, but Steinbrenner believed he could control anyone.

Man on the Move

Martin had been a scrappy star of Yankee championship clubs of the 1950s, a buddy of Mickey Mantle and Whitey Ford, a pet of manager Casey Stengel. He was traded by general manager George Weiss after being involved in a fight in a New York nightclub and counted the days until he could return to his beloved "Big Town."

As manager in Minnesota in 1969, he took a seventh-place team to first place, in his first season, but was fired after he had a fight with one of his pitchers outside a saloon. He went to Detroit, where he took a fourth-place team to first place in his second season, but was fired after a series of arguments with management.

In Texas, he took a sixth-place team to second place by his second season before being fired after a series of arguments with the management there. He thought he'd blown his last chance until Steinbrenner and the Yankees signed him later in the season to return to New York, where he was a living legend and a favorite of the fans.

You could win with him, but could you live with him? "I don't know if I can change," admitted Martin, "but I'm happy to be home." He considered the Yankees his family, but he was not much of a family man.

He fought with the front office for the type of players he wanted and he drove his players hard, using kicks in the pants more than pats on the back. He was a fiery fellow who freely criticized players and popped off a lot. He put a lot of pressure on his players, but got a lot out of them.

His best player was his captain, Thurman Munson, a skilled catcher and all-around athlete who looked like the fat man at a picnic who pretends he can play ball. A gruff guy who seldom showed a smile behind his walrus mustache, Munson liked to needle his teammates and insult reporters. He hated the spotlight, but liked to get a lot of credit. He was Martin's kind of player. Jackson wasn't. Jackson was Steinbrenner's player.

Munson was the leader of the Yankees; Jackson liked to be the leader. There was bound to be conflict between the two. And a scramble for the spotlight among Jackson, Martin, and Steinbrenner was inevitable.

There was bound to be a clash of big egos and considerable controversy when these temperamental, outspoken characters came together on one team. But it also was bound to be quite a team.

7

Yankee Dandy

It is easier for the big teams to pay the big salaries to players than most people realize. Take the Yankees, for example. They drew more than two million fans in 1976 and again in 1977, both at home and on the road. They kept 80 percent at home and received 20 percent on the road. This produced about $8 million in ticket money. Food and other concessions at home brought in another $4 million. Television and radio rights were worth about $3 million. Other rights brought in another $1 million. The gross was more than $16 million each year.

Of course, the club had considerable expenses. The cost of operating the team at home and on the road and running the stadium was about $5 million. The city rented the stadium to the team for about $1 million. The player payroll rose from about $3 million in 1976 to about $4 million in 1977. However, this still was only about one fourth of the gross receipts and less than one half of the expenses. The team's net profit probably was more than $5 million.

However, many major league teams are losers and lose money. Steinbrenner said, "We lost money for a few years before we began to make money. And we have put our profits back into the franchise to improve it. It is a valuable asset. The more valuable it is, the more money we can get for it if we ever sell it. We take the long-range view of our investment. We do not need to take money out of it to live on every year. The only thing we need to do every year is put a competitive team on the field which will win more than the next team.

"Winning is the most important thing, not only because it brings in the fans and brings in profits, but because I am by nature a very competitive person who needs to win to be happy and am very unhappy when we are losing," he concluded. "I have paid a lot of money for a manager who knows how to win and top players who should win and I will be very unhappy if we do not win it all this year."

Despite having won the team's first pennant in five years the previous season, the Yankees' loss of four straight games in the World Series left the owner deeply disappointed, and he determined to drive his club to a championship in 1977. He spent freely to pick up not only Jackson, but also pitcher Don Gullet in the free-agent market. He authorized deals by which team president Gabe Paul acquired pitcher Mike Torrez, shortstop Bucky Dent, and outfielders Cliff Johnson and Paul Blair.

The Yankees went into the season with Chris Chambliss on first base, Willie Randolph on second base, Dent at shortstop, and Graig Nettles on third base; Jackson, Mickey Rivers, and Lou Piniella or Roy White in the outfield, and Thurman Munson behind home plate. Piniella, White, and Johnson shared designated-hitter duties. Gullett, Torrez, Ed Figueroa, and Catfish Hunter were the starters. Gullet and Hunter suffered from sore arms all season, on and off. Ron Guidry, a twenty-six-year-old veteran of the minor leagues who had failed to make the majors in two previous seasons, was pressed into service. Sparky Lyle was the relief ace of a rather thin bullpen staff.

Reggie was supposed to be the hitter the team needed to take the title. Munson, the captain of the team, supported the addition of Jackson. Steinbrenner brought Munson to the press conference announcing the signing of Jackson and said, "Thurman played a major role in our decision to go after Reggie. Gabe Paul wanted to go after Bobby Grich instead. But I was always a Jackson man and Munson encouraged me."

Munson said, "I felt we needed a left-handed power-hitter and an outfielder who could throw. Jackson fills the bill. I'm thinking of the team."

But then, Munson started thinking of himself. When he found out that Jackson was making more money than he, Munson was furious. He had accepted the fact that Steinbrenner had to go high to get Hunter, but the owner had assured him that no other player would make more. Steinbrenner assured him his contract would be adjusted appropriately when the time came to renew it, but Munson was dissatisfied. He went to spring training resentful of Reggie.

In spring training, all of the players held themselves apart from Reggie. They watched him and waited to see how he would work out. All of the media attention centered on Reggie, naturally, and the players resented this. He strutted a little and they didn't like this. Of course, that is the way he is. He told the writers, "I'm the big fish and now I'm in the big pond. I've got a big job to do, but I've got the big bat to do it with.

"All I read is that I'm supposed to create controversy. I don't look for it. It follows me around. I can live with it. I've learned how to handle it."

Reggie wipes the sweat from his brow following a hot pre-game workout. *(Author's collection)*

In spring training Reggie gave an interview to a writer, Robert Ward, from *Sport* magazine, in which he said he was the key that would unlock the door to success for the Yankees—"the straw that stirs the drink." He said Munson was a winner, "but there's just nobody who can do for a club what I can do." He said he would be the leader Munson had not been.

"He's being so damned insecure about the whole thing," Reggie said of Thurman. "I'll hear him telling some writer that he wants it to be known that he's captain of the team, that he knows what's best. Stuff like that. And when somebody knocks me, he'll laugh real loud so I can hear it." When asked if he should talk it over with Thurman, Reggie said, "No, he's not ready for it yet."

Early in the season, when the story broke, Munson and most of the other Yankees were bitter about it. Their coolness to Jackson turned into a deep freeze. Munson was not an easy man to like. He was gruff and tough. When he spoke to reporters he was sarcastic. But he talked to his teammates, and they respected his toughness as a player. They sided with him, against Jackson. They were not talking to Reggie, so he was not talking to them.

After he hit a home run in one game, they went to the lip of the dugout and extended their hands to shake his when he returned. It was the customary thing to do. But he ignored them and went to the other end of the dugout without shaking their hands. Later he said, "I have a hurt hand." Asked about it, Munson said, "He's a liar."

Reggie is a bit of a braggart at times. He should not have said some of the things he said in that magazine article. The A's had become accustomed to him and just shrugged such things off. The A's knew what he would do for them. The Yankees did not. They were not used to his ways and could not overlook them. Catfish Hunter said, "You have to get to know Reggie. You have to know that he needs to be known as the best, he needs to lead. He may be the best. He can lead. But he's got to show this team, not tell it."

Reggie was wearing the Yankee uniform, but he was not yet a part of the team. He felt alone among his teammates. He admitted later, "It was a very hard time for me. I was on a new team in a new town and I felt unloved and lonely." He got off to a slow start. He hit a few home runs, but did not hit consistently. He dropped a few fly balls. He was not earning his enormous salary and the players resented this.

It was Billy Martin's job as manager to pull the team together, but Billy had his own troubles. When the team lost five straight games and eight of its first ten, Steinbrenner got on Billy's back. Both denied reports the owner was trying to dictate lineups to the manager, but it came out later that Steinbrenner kept asking Martin to bat Jackson in the fourth, the cleanup, slot.

Munson had batted cleanup the previous season and wanted to stay there. Jackson was used to batting cleanup and wanted to be there. Martin solved the problem by batting Munson third and Jackson fifth, and batting Chambliss cleanup. Steinbrenner talked to or telephoned Martin with advice constantly. Billy got angry about it and after one call ripped the telephone off the wall. Later, Martin publicly criticized Steinbrenner for not giving him an extra catcher and the owner fined him $2,500.

The team did have talent and went on a tear, winning nine of 11, including six straight. Chambliss drove in five runs in one game, six in another. Booed on his return to Baltimore, Reggie responded with a home run and two doubles. However, Reggie got only one hit in 25 times at bat early in May and was benched for a few games. Meanwhile, Munson hit in 16 straight games and drove in 21 runs during May. The Yankees went on another tear, winning seven of eight, to stay tight with Baltimore and Boston in the race for the divisional lead. At month's end, the Yankees were 26–21 and 1½ games out of first place.

Through mid-June, Ed Figueroa was the hot Yankee starter and Sparky Lyle the hot reliever. Ron Guidry was starting effectively and in mid-June he pitched the first complete game and the first shutout of his brief big league career. Munson drove in five runs in five games early in the month, and when he went out with an injury, Reggie started to hit with consistency and carried the attack for a while. At mid-month, the Yankees had moved into the divisional lead, but they fell from first when they lost three straight in Boston in a controversial series that almost tore the team apart.

The Red Sox had an awesome array of hitters, including Jim Rice, Carl Yastrzemski, Fred Lynn, George Scott, Butch Hobson, and Carlton Fisk. They had fair pitchers, including Luis Tiant, Bill Lee, Ferguson Jenkins, Rick Wise, and relief ace Bill Campbell. But it was power that produced most of their victories. They went on a home run tear to put the Yankees to rout in the three games in their little Fenway Park and knock the New Yorkers out of first place. But it was the middle game of the set that was most meaningful.

In the nationally televised game of Saturday afternoon, June 18, Rice hit a sinking line drive that Reggie could not catch. Looking at it over and over again on replays, it looks as if Reggie merely misplays the ball. But Martin felt he had not hustled on the play. Right then and there he sent out a substitute to replace Reggie. Embarrassed, Jackson stormed off the field and into the dugout. He and Martin cursed each other and threatened to throw punches at one another.

Martin raged hysterically at Reggie and had to be held back by Yogi Berra and other coaches and players from getting at him. Most of the threatening moves were made by Martin. The intensity of Martin's temper tantrum startled Jackson and he just stood there stunned, as though confronted by a madman. Cameras caught all of the argument and the incident was replayed several times. It was an enormously embarrassing incident for the proud Yankees.

Later, Martin said, "If a player doesn't hustle and he shows the club up, then I'll show him up. Words

Reggie Jackson charges into New York Yankee dugout at Boston's Fenway Park, June 18, 1977, as manager Billy Martin moves out to meet him in historic confrontation. Martin had pulled Jackson out of nationally televised Saturday afternoon game for "failing to hustle" in the field, and their argument touched off shock waves which are still stirring. *(AP photo)*

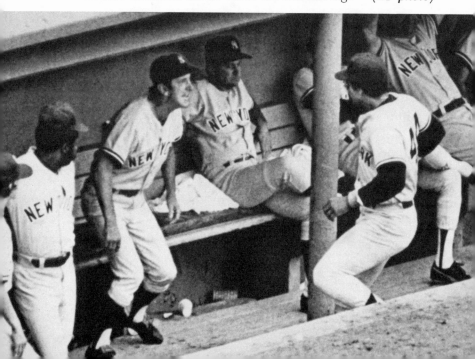

were said that I didn't like. Then he challenged management when he tried to take a punch at me. What was I supposed to do, let him get away with it?" Jackson said, "I charged the ball the way I thought I could play it best. If Martin feels I didn't hustle, I feel sorry for him. You know, in this game, the manager is always right. I'm just a player."

Later, Reggie added, "It makes me cry the way they treat me on this team. They treat me like a nigger. The Yankee pinstripes are Ruth and Gehrig and DiMaggio and Mantle. The Yankee Hall of Famers have all been white. I'm just a black man to them, who doesn't know how to be subservient. I'm a black man with an IQ of 160 making $600,000 a year and they treat me like dirt. They've never had anyone like me on their team before."

They had not.

Munson said, "The whole thing makes me sick."

It made Steinbrenner sick, too. He had not been at the game, but was told about the incident by Gabe Paul. Paul immediately met with Martin and Jackson and announced, "The trouble is resolved." Martin said, "Everything is fine." Jackson said, "It's all over."

But it wasn't.

Steinbrenner flew to Detroit to meet with Martin and Paul. He was going to fire Martin, but Paul talked him out of it. The owner felt the manager had lost control of the team and himself and had behaved badly in a way that had cost him managerial jobs before. But Paul convinced him that the owner would not want it to look as if Jackson had won over management.

Instead, Steinbrenner made a statement that embarrassed Billy badly. He said, "Martin is the best manager in baseball and the Yankees want to have the best. But we were headed for complete collapse. Dissension on the team was terrible. We were getting no leadership. I told Billy he had to pay more attention to his responsibilities immediately. He was very subdued and promised to get in touch with me every day. I intend to keep in daily contact with the team."

He laid down a set of seven rules he expected the manager to follow, though they never were revealed. He acted like a teacher reprimanding a rebellious student. Then he went to Jackson and he told Reggie he didn't know if he was right or wrong in the incident, but that he was no racist and if Reggie ever blamed racism for his problems with the team again he'd "tear his head off." Then he went to Munson and told him he was not providing the leadership a captain should. Thurman said, "I thought Reggie was the captain." Steinbrenner said, "When I want Reggie to be the captain, I'll name him captain. You're the captain. Now be the captain."

The Yankees had lost two straight to Detroit to run their losing streak to five in a row and had fallen five games out of first place. Munson was saying he wanted to be traded to Cleveland, near his home in Ohio. Mickey Rivers was asking to be traded anywhere. Jackson was saying, "You'll never see me in a Yankee uniform again after this season." Torrez was complaining he wasn't being pitched enough. Everyone was complaining about this or that. There was bickering on the bench and in the clubhouse.

Steinbrenner's tirade seemed to set a lot of them straight. Martin was subdued. Munson and Jackson were subdued. Reggie said, "There's been too much talk and not enough action. We have talent and it's time to show it on the field. We're professionals and it's time to do the job."

A three-run home run by Graig Nettles and a two-run triple by Jackson produced a 12–10 triumph over the Tigers and ended the Yankees' losing streak. Then the team returned home to sweep a three-game series from the Red Sox before roaring crowds of more than 55,000 fans. Munson had six hits in the three games.

The turning point in the pennant race may have come in the first game. The Yankees were losing, 5–3, with two out and no one on base in the last of the ninth. Willie Randolph tripled and Roy White hit a home run to tie the game. Jackson pinch-hit a single to win it in the 11th.

Cliff Johnson and Lou Piniella went on a hitting spree. Johnson hit three home runs in the last game of June. The Yankees won 16 of their last 18 games that month and ended the month with a 42–33 record, back in first place by a half game over Boston and by three games over Baltimore.

However, there were too many temperamental people on that team for it to proceed smoothly. The Yankees opened July by losing three straight games at home to Detroit. Guidry stopped the skid by pitching his second shutout and the Yankees then won four straight from Cleveland. Torrez began to get regular starts and pitched well. Munson put together another hitting streak of 12 games. He knocked in two runs in one game with a home run and two more with a single as the Yankees won the opener of a big four-game series with the Orioles in Baltimore. But the Orioles then won the last three in a row.

The Yankees lost three straight to the Royals. They won the opener of a series with the Brewers, but then lost the next two to fall into third place, three games back. They lost a lead in the ninth inning of one game and were playing poorly. Steinbrenner flew into Milwaukee to meet with Martin. He talked to him, then went to bed and thought about firing him.

Munson and Piniella knocked on his door. He got up and let them in and they told him the team could not win with Martin as manager. Then Martin knocked on the door. He'd heard that the players were talking to the owner behind his back. The four argued until after four in the morning.

Steinbrenner decided that his players could not tell him what to do. Stubbornly, he decided not to fire his manager. He did tell Martin he thought the team would do better with Jackson at cleanup, Piniella as designated hitter, and his best four starters in a regular rotation. Stubbornly, Martin said he'd think about it.

The Orioles led by three games when they came to Yankee Stadium for a three-game series late in the month. The Yankees trailed, 4–2, in the ninth inning of the first game. Cliff Johnson hit a two-run pinch-hit home run to tie the game. Jackson then hit a home run to win it, 5–4, in the 11th. After losing the middle game, the Yankees bounced back to bomb Baltimore, 14–2, in the final game, the last of the season between the two contenders.

Somehow, these Yankees came back every time they were being counted out. They won eight of their final nine games in July to finish the month only one game behind Baltimore and Boston.

Early in August, the Yankees lost four out of five games to fall five games out of first place again. Opening a home stand on the 10th of the month, Martin finally followed Steinbrenner's wishes, inserted Jackson into the cleanup role, put Piniella in as designated hitter, went to a four-man pitching rotation, and the Yankees went on a streak of 13 victories in 14 games.

On the 16th, the White Sox were losing by five runs in the ninth inning of a game at Yankee Stadium when they scored six runs to take the lead, but the Yankees came back in the home half on a two-run home run by Chambliss to win the game and keep the team's spirits soaring. Exactly one week later, on the 23rd, the Yankees whipped the White Sox again to take over first place again.

As it turned out, they were to stay this time.

Jackson started to hit with terrific power and in tight spots. Munson got back on the beam with his bat. Rivers ripped the ball at a .400 pace and drove home 21 runs during the month. The Yankees won 21 of their last 24 games in August to move four games ahead of Boston and Baltimore with an 80–52 season record. Suddenly they looked like the team they were supposed to be.

Winning seemed to make everyone happy and the Yankees started to act like teammates. Munson and Jackson talked to each other once in a while. They seemed to have reached a grudging respect for each other. Munson had played in pain all season, but played well with injuries. And Jackson was coming through when it counted, as he always did. He hit 10 home runs and drove in 29 runs during the month. The other players respected this and thawed toward Reggie a little. He was warmed by his success.

The Yankees won six of their first eight games in September. They had a bad series with Toronto, losing two out of three, one by 19–3, and went into a crucial

142

series with Boston with the lead in jeopardy. More than 54,000 fans filled Yankee Stadium for each game of the series.

The Yankees won the opener, 4–2, behind a two-run home run by Rivers and five-hit pitching by Guidry. They won the second game, 2–0, behind seven-hit pitching by Figueroa, a two-run home run by Reggie, and two spectacular outfield catches by Reggie.

Boston won the final game, 7–3, despite home runs by Jackson and Munson, but the Red Sox had lost the games they needed to win. A week later, the Red Sox won two from the Yankees in Boston, but it was too late.

Baltimore had fallen from the race with an awful August, and although the Orioles came on again in September, it was too late.

The Yankees won six straight games and nine out of 11 late in the month to protect their lead. Jackson hit a grand slam home run to crush Cleveland on the night of the 28th to clinch a tie for the title.

The next night, Boston lost to Baltimore and the Yankees were in. They lost that night, but it didn't matter. They celebrated taking the divisional title with a champagne celebration in their dressing room.

Jackson, a bottle of champagne in one hand, threw his other arm around Martin. Martin said to Jackson, "I'm proud of you." Jackson said, "I'll drink to that."

Jackson drank. Then Martin took the bottle from Jackson and drank. Then Jackson went to embrace Munson.

All of a sudden, they were together as a team as they headed for the championship playoffs. Or so it seemed. They still had differences.

Martin said, "It had to be the hardest year of my baseball life. A lot of it was sour, but winning was sweet. It makes up for most of our troubles. If we can win this with all the troubles we've had, we can win it all.

"The turning point came when I stood up to Reggie in the dugout after he dogged it on that play in Boston back in June. I had to show the team that I was the boss, that I couldn't be pushed around by a player or ordered around by an owner.

"All I ask is that the owner show me a little respect. This was a tough team to manage. I held it together. He almost cost us the pennant. I won despite him and now he's going to find it very hard to fire me."

Angered in what should have been a moment of joy, Steinbrenner said, "We put this team together without him. We got him the best team money could buy. He's crazy to take credit for our success. The credit should go to the players like Jackson who came through for us.

"The turning point came when Martin made Jackson the cleanup hitter. I'd been after him to make that change for a long time. From the time he did, we

144

were almost unbeatable. Whether he'll admit it or not, Martin has changed. He'll listen now."

From that point, the Yankees had won 41 of 53 games to regain the divisional lead and pull away from the others. Jackson drove in 49 runs in those final 53 games. He wound up with 110 runs batted in. He tied his career high with 39 doubles and wound up with 32 home runs.

He struck out 129 times to increase to 10 seasons his league record for leading the league in this, but his .286 batting average was one of the highest of his career, and his slugging average of .550 was among the best in baseball.

Reggie did make 13 errors, second highest among outfielders in the league.

He led the team in RBIs, while Nettles had 107, Munson 100, and Johnson 90. Nettles led in home runs with 37, while Munson had 19. Piniella had the best batting average at .330, while Rivers had .326 and Munson .308.

Torrez led in pitching victories with 17, but lost 13. Figueroa was 16–11, Guidry 16–7. Guidry came through in the clutch, winning 10 of his last 12 decisions, Gullett was 14–4, but sidelined by September. Lyle won 13 and saved 26 in a brilliant relief role which would win him Cy Young Award honors.

Responding to the pressure superbly, Reggie really might have been Most Valuable Player in the league again, but Lyle, Munson, and he divided the Yankee votes and finished sixth, seventh and eighth, respectively. The laurels went to Rod Carew of lowly Minnesota. Reggie didn't seem to mind.

"I'm just happy the team won," he sighed. "No one will ever know the misery I went through. I never want to go through it again. I don't know how much of it was my fault, but I know I never felt as alone or was as lonely.

"I sent my girl friend home. I wouldn't let my father come to games. My mother developed a heart condition so she couldn't come to games. My family was sick over the way I was treated. But I feel like I came through when it counted. I take pride in producing under pressure and give thanks to God for giving me the strength to overcome my own faults and all obstacles in my way."

The Yankees had won 100 games, lost only 62, and finished three games in front of both Boston and Baltimore, but now a new season was starting, the postseason, and they had to prove themselves anew.

On the eve of the opener of the American League pennant playoffs, Martin announced that he deserved a new contract. After taking the pennant the previous season, he had signed a contract for three years at $250,000 a year. Now he wanted one for five years at $500,000 a year. "What's money to George?" he laughed.

George didn't find it funny. "This is no time to be talking contract," Steinbrenner said. "This is the time to be thinking about beating Kansas City in the play-offs and going on to win the World Series. Billy seems to forget we lost the World Series in four straight games last season."

He spoke as if he would not hesitate to fire Martin if his team did not win it all this season, no matter what Martin thought. "I'll let him go, win or lose, any time he is hurting my team," he warned.

The best-of-five series opened with two games in front of 55,000-fan crowds in Yankee Stadium.

Martin gambled on Gullett in the opener, and Don, who had been out much of the season with a sore shoulder, lasted less than two innings. Four home runs helped the Royals to a romp, 7–2, despite a home run by Munson.

In the second game, the two teams swapped the lead back and forth to a 2–2 tie after six innings. Hal McRae sent Willie Randolph flying with a football block on a force-out at second base and the two teams began to snap and snarl at each other.

The Yankees went on to win, 6–2, to even the series with two runs coming in on a two-out error by George Brett when the ball went between the third baseman's legs. Guidry gave up only three hits in winning the biggest game of his brief career.

Jackson singled and scored the last run, but it

turned out to be his only hit of the first four games. Munson was blanked for the first time in 11 post-season games in the third game, at Kansas City, as the Royals raced to a 6–2 victory. Dennis Leonard outpitched Torrez.

The Yankees were within one game of defeat as they faced the last two games in Kansas City. Martin admitted, "Our backs are to the wall, but we've battled back before." Jackson said, "This club has shown it has a strong character and can overcome a lot. We're a lot like the A's were. We can win, as they did."

Figueroa faced Larry Gura in the fourth game. Rivers doubled and singled and Dent doubled in two early surges as the Yankees went ahead, 3–0. Munson doubled and Piniella singled him home to make it 4–0 in the third. In the home half, Patek tripled, Hal McRae singled, and Brett tripled to make it 4–2.

Nettles singled in a run in the fourth and it was 5–2. But Patek doubled to key a Royal rally that made it 5–4 in the home half. Lyle relieved and blanked the Royals the rest of the way. Rivers got his fourth hit of the game and wound up scoring the last run as the Yankees won, 6–4, to square the series.

Going into the fifth and final game, Jackson was 1-for-14 and Chambliss 1-for-13. It is not clear why Martin did not bench Chambliss, but he decided to bench Reggie. Martin said, "It's the most difficult decision I ever made, but he's not hitting and we have to try someone else."

Steinbrenner said, "He's the manager. If he wins, he takes the credit. If he loses, he has to be blamed."

Jackson said, "I can't hit if I don't play, but I haven't been hitting and I respect his right to make a move. I can't make myself believe Billy would do this out of spite. It's hard to take but I can take it like a man." He rooted for the team from the bench during the game.

Martin said, "He showed me something with that. He showed me a lot of class."

The turnout of more than 40,000 fans screamed when Rivers misplayed Brett's fly ball to center in the first inning. Racing into third, Brett crashed into Nettles. As they went down, Nettles kicked at Brett. They came up punching. Nettles suffered a sore shoulder. And the home side took a 2–0 lead.

The Yankees picked up a run in the third as Rivers singled, stole second, and scored on Munson's single. But the Royals made it 3–1 in the home half as McRae doubled and Cowens singled. Torrez replaced Guidry at that point. And Torrez and Paul Splitorff dueled scorelessly for four innings after that.

However, when Randolph opened the eighth with a single, Herzog brought in Doug Bird. He did strike out Munson. But Piniella singled Randolph to third. And Martin sent up Jackson to pinch-hit. With his superb sense of the dramatic, Reggie singled in the run that made it 3–2.

Steve Mingori came in to get Nettles on a fly ball.

But Chambliss then ripped what looked like the game-tying hit up the middle. However, second baseman Frank White made an incredible diving stop of the ball and flipped to Patek to force the runner out at second. The lead had been saved and the Kansas City fans stood and cheered.

Still, these Yankees had courage. They had won in the last inning of the last game by coming from behind on a Chambliss homer against the Royals the year before, and determined now to pull out another dramatic triumph.

Reggie's replacement, Paul Blair, opened with a single. White walked. And Rivers singled in the tying run.

Randolph's fly ball scored White with the lead run. Munson's ground-out brought Rivers to third. And, when Piniella's grounder was thrown into the outfield by the erratic third-baseman Brett, Mickey came in to make it 5–3. Lyle, hurling relief, retired the Royals in order in the last of the ninth.

Patek made the last out and the little fellow, smallest man in the majors at 5-4, stood in frustrated disappointment at first base, head down, as the joyous Yankees raced off, whooping and hollering.

Some 3,000 fans welcomed the club home at Newark Airport. Rivers had led the Yankees with nine hits in the playoff, but Munson was the hero with six hits and five runs driven in. He now had 25 hits and 10

RBI's in two playoffs and one World Series. He said, "We will not be 0-for-4 in this World Series."

Jackson said, "Not with Mr. October in the lineup. That's me. If Martin puts me back in, I'll hit." Martin said, "He's going back in. We're going with our best. We're the best and we'll prove it."

They had to prove it to the Los Angeles Dodgers, who had ended the Reds' domination of major league baseball by beating them out in the National League West, then topped Philadelphia in the pennant play-off.

The Dodgers were led by a colorful, cocky rookie manager, Tommy Lasorda, who said, "We'll win because God has Dodger blue blood." If they won, how-ever, it would be because they had deep pitching and plenty of power, despite an ordinary defense.

The series opened before 56,668 fans at Yankee Stadium. Short on starters, Martin turned to sore-armed Don Gullett. After a shaky start, he dueled Dodger ace Don Sutton on even terms.

A triple by Bill Russell helped the Dodgers to a 2–0 lead in the first inning. The Yankees got one back in the home half when, with two out, Munson, Jackson, and Chambliss singled in succession. Light-hitting Randolph tied it with a homer in the sixth. And Mun-son doubled in the lead run in the eighth.

The Dodgers had only four hits off Gullett when Dusty Baker opened the ninth with a single. Mota flied out, but Steve Yeager walked and Martin turned to his ace, Lyle. He gave up a game-scoring single to Lee Lacy, but nothing more after that. Rick Rhoden was pitching in the 12th inning when Randolph doubled and Blair, who had replaced Reggie on defense, came through with a game-winning single.

The Dodgers evened the series in the second game, 6–1, as Burt Hooten stopped the Yankees on five hits. Martin made a controversial move by starting sore-shouldered Hunter and the Catfish was blasted for three runs in three innings before he was removed.

Later, Reggie supported his old pal by asking, "How could Martin start him when he hasn't pitched for more than a month? It wasn't fair to him." Martin said, "He's paid to play and I'm paid to manage. If he doesn't like my decisions he can kiss my butt."

Steinbrenner brought them together. After they met, Martin said, "We've talked it over and we're together on this." Jackson said, "Maybe I was out of line, but the Catfish had been my teammate for ten years and I thought someone should speak in his defense. He's come through for me and I thought I should come through for him."

Hunter sighed and said, "I didn't want him butting into it, but that's the way he is. He doesn't think before he speaks, but he will do anything for a friend. Whatever else he is, he is faithful to his friends. Whatever he does, he means well."

Munson said, "We have a chance to win a World Series and one guy's second-guessing the manager. I guess Billy just doesn't realize Reggie's 'Mr. October.' I read that somewhere. I'm fed up. This stuff just doesn't stop. I guarantee you, after this series I'm gone. I'll never be back here. I don't know how we win."

But they do win.

And they keep coming back.

In Los Angeles for the third game, the Yankees settled the issue swiftly. They took a 3–0 lead in the first inning on doubles by Rivers and Munson and singles by Jackson and Piniella off Tommy John.

The Dodgers tied it in the third on a three-run home run by Baker off Torrez, but Mike blanked the Dodgers the rest of the way.

Singles by Nettles and Dent helped the Yankees to the lead run in the fourth. Jackson walked and scored the final run in the fifth on singles by Piniella and Chambliss to wrap it up at 5–3.

The Yankees made it three out of four the following afternoon as Guidry stopped the Dodgers on four hits and two runs, a two-run home run by Dangerous Davey Lopes.

The Yankees had led, 3–0, after Jackson doubled, Piniella singled, Chambliss doubled, and Dent singled in the second.

Piniella protected the 3–2 lead in the fourth when

he leaped above the left-field wall to rob Ron Cey of a home run.

And Jackson wrapped it up in the sixth at 4–2 when he drove a home run over that wall.

The Dodgers stayed alive by winning the fifth game, 10–4, clobbering Gullett and a couple of relievers with 13 hits, including home runs by Yeager and Smith.

The Yankees got nine hits, including home runs by Munson and Jackson, but the blows came after Sutton was coasting along on a large lead. Jackson's home run came in his last time at bat.

So the two teams went back to Yankee Stadium. And Gabe Paul announced that Martin had been given a new contract and a new car by the boss. Gracefully, Billy said, "I'm grateful, but all I'm thinking about now is winning this thing. The pressure's still on me." Reggie grinned and said, "I love the pressure."

It was Torrez versus Hooten in the sixth game before 56,407 fans and a multimillion-person television audience on this fateful Tuesday night.

An error by Dent, a walk, and a two-out triple by Garvey gave the Dodgers a 2–0 lead in the first. A walk to Jackson and a home run by Chambliss tied it in the second. A home run by Smith gave the Dodgers a 3–2 lead in the third.

A single by Munson, the tenth consecutive World Series game in which he had hit safely, and a home run by Jackson, his third of the Series, made it 4–3. A double by Chambliss, a ground out, and a fly out made it 5–3 before the fourth was finished.

Reggie had homered off Sutton on his last swing in his last at-bat the previous game. The walk his first time up in this game did not count as an at-bat. His homer his second time up off Hooten came on a first pitch, giving him two home runs in his last two swings.

With the smile of success on his face, Reggie hits the second of his three home runs on three pitches in the sixth and final game of the 1977 World Series victory over the Los Angeles Dodgers. *(Wide World Photos)*

In the fifth, Elia Sosa was pitching. Rivers singled and was forced at second. Munson flied out. With two out, Reggie swung on Sosa's first pitch and drove it on a line into the right-field stands. It was his second home run of the game and third on three pitches in two games.

It was a dramatic moment and the fans came to their feet and applauded and cheered as Reggie rounded the bases. His two-run blast seemed to have settled the issue and the World Series at 7–3.

His teammates, Martin and Munson included, came to the dugout steps to stick their hands out to him. He shook their hands and slapped palms with them and happily accepted their pats on the back and shouts of congratulations.

The Dodgers seemed stunned.

There was great excitement in the air as Reggie came to bat again to lead off the eighth. Charlie Hough was pitching. It seemed beyond reason that Reggie could hit another one, but on Hough's first pitch, Reggie swung and drove the ball into the bleachers in center field.

It was an unbelievable moment, and Dodger Steve Garvey could not help applauding as Reggie rounded first base, a big grin on his face, the fans standing and hollering for him, all of the world that was watching overwhelmed by what he had done. Four pitches by four different pitchers and four straight home runs!

Yankee Dandy

Reggie was the sort of hero he had always wanted to be and he seemed to float on air as he rounded the bases and headed home to another round of congratulations by his excited teammates. Munson was among the first to take his hand.

In his joy, Reggie paced up and down the dugout, shaking his fist triumphantly in front of him. He had to step out of the dugout briefly to tip his cap to the crowd, which demanded another appearance.

All wound up, shaking clenched fists in triumph, Jackson stalks into the Yankee clubhouse following another of his four straight home runs and three in a row in the winning game of the '77 World Series. *(Wide World Photos)*

He received yet a third standing ovation when he took the field for the final inning. And when the final out was made, he had to race through a broken field of fans who had stormed the field and block one away from him like the football player he used to be as he headed for the dressing room.

Here he was hugged by Steinbrenner and a weeping Martin and he poured champagne over Munson. The Dodgers were done in in six games and the Yankees were world champions again for the first time in fifteen years. More than any other player, Reggie was responsible.

Munson admitted it: "I've got to give it to him. He came through in the stretch and he came through in the World Series. Winning it makes up for a lot." Martin admitted, "Reggie won it for us and I'm grateful to him. After what we went through, this is the thrill of my life."

Steinbrenner said, "He's the hero. He did what I thought he would do for us. He won it for us as he won it for the A's."

Even in the dismal dressing room of the Dodgers there was awe and admiration for Reggie. Lasorda said, "He did it to us and I've never seen anything like it." Garvey said, "He has to go down with the greats."

Reggie's three home runs matched the one-game record set by Babe Ruth in two earlier World Series

The MVP of the 1977 World Series, former football star turned baseball star Reggie Jackson is about to throw a block on a fan as he races to safety through the crowd that swarmed on the field following last out of 1977 final game.

(Wide World Photos)

of more than forty years back. His four straight set a new record for a World Series. His five in the Series surpassed the four of Ruth, Gehrig, and three others. His ten runs scored was another record, and he drove in eight. He had nine hits and set another record with 25 total bases. Told some of this, he smiled and said, "The word 'superstar' is used too often for too many players, but this one time, at least, I guess I do belong with the greats."

Others contributed, too, of course. Munson had

eight hits to give him 17 in ten games over two World Series and 33 hits over 20 games in four post-season series. Few ever produced under pressure so successfully.

Jackson was one who did. He had to be, as he was, voted Most Valuable Player of a World Series for the second time, the first one ever to win the honor twice.

He received his trophy and a new car at ceremonies in New York a couple of days later. He received the cheers of the crowd and he grinned gratefully and said, "I've got to admit it was not an easy season for me and for my team, but winning makes it worthwhile. I've been part of four championship teams now and each one is equally satisfying.

"A lot of us said we wouldn't be back in the heat of all that went on with us this season, but I think those of us they'll have back will all be back next season. When you're with a winner, you don't like to leave. I'm going home to California to enjoy the winter right now, but I'll be back to try to win another next season."

If he felt revenge was his, he did not say so. If he was happy to be the hero, he accepted the gifts of victory gracefully.

160

8

The Comeback Kings

Entering the new season, the world champion New York Yankees almost unanimously agreed there would be no repeat of the controversies surrounding the club in 1977 and there would be smooth sailing in 1978.

On reporting to spring training, Reggie Jackson said, "Last year there was a lot of pressure to prove to myself and everyone else that I was worth the kind of money I was making. I proved it. Every year you have to prove yourself all over again, but I don't feel the tension now that I felt then.

161

As befits a man earning $600,000 a year, Reggie Jackson keeps warm in a new fur coat he has just purchased as he strolls in Manhattan in fall of 1977. *(Wide World Photos)*

"Since the World Series, people respect me. I feel George Steinbrenner, Billy Martin, Thurman Munson, and my other teammates respect me. I respect them. I guess we had to get to know one another and our ways. We went through a lot together and that brought us together. I think we will be a real team this year.

"I don't want any hassles this season. I don't want to say anything anyone will take wrong. I just want to play ball. I just want to win. I just want to enjoy myself."

Billy Martin said, "I don't think there's going to be much controversy this season. We got a lot of misunderstandings out of our system last season."

A few were not so sure.

Thurman Munson spent the off-season trying to be traded to Ohio, swearing he would not return to the Yankees. George Steinbrenner satisfied him with a new contract comparable to Reggie's, and Thurman returned.

"Nothing's changed," he growled. "I'm surrounded by the same idiots. I'm not so sure there won't be the same hassles, I'd still like to leave. I never said I wouldn't come back, but I'd still like to leave.

"And from now on I haven't got anything to say to anyone."

And George Steinbrenner smiled and said, "I'll trade who I want to trade. I won't trade who I don't want to trade. I don't expect everyone to be happy. I like a little commotion in my life and on my team. It makes you tough."

Lou Piniella added, "Hell, no, it won't be any better. We have the same people. And we'll have the same troubles."

He was right, except the people were not all the same.

Gabe Paul left to take over the Cleveland Indians. And Al Rosen, a former Cleveland Indian and an old favorite of the owner's, took over as Steinbrenner's right-hand man.

Steinbrenner dipped into the free-agent market to acquire relief pitchers Rich Gossage and Rawly Eastwick. At that point, relief ace Sparky Lyle asked, "How many relief pitchers can a team use?"

The answer was one. Sparky was used less than any healthy Cy Young Award-winner in history. Eastwick didn't last long and soon went on his way. The hard-throwing Gossage became the bullpen star.

When Mike Torrez went to the Red Sox via the free-agent route, Steinbrenner brought in Andy Messersmith from Atlanta, but he soon was slowed by a sore arm and saw little action. Don Gullett remained a sore-arm case and saw little action.

Ron Guidry became the ace of the staff, followed by Ed Figueroa. Dick Tidrow came out of the bullpen to become a starter. Big Jim Beattie was brought up from the minors to become a starter. Catfish Hunter came off the injured list to return to the rotation.

The starting lineup remained much the same, with Chambliss, Randolph, Dent, and Nettles in the infield, Munson behind the plate, and Rivers, Jackson, and Piniella or White in the outfield. Early on, Jackson became primarily the designated hitter with Piniella, White, or Gary Thomasson filling in.

Reggie didn't like it at all. But he had been betrayed by his glove.

His bat remained a lethal weapon and on his first trip to the plate in the 1978 season opener, on the

Number 44, right-fielder Reggie Jackson, doffs his cap to cheering fans following another big hit under pressure in Yankee Stadium. *(Wide World Photos)*

14th of April, he hit his fifth straight home run. The game had to be delayed five minutes as 44,678 fans, who had been given new "Reggie" candy bars free, showered many of them on the field in tribute to him.

The pitcher was Wilbur Wood of the White Sox and the pitch was his first to Reggie, making him the fifth consecutive victim of Jackson's slugging prowess on five consecutive pitches. Five months and 26 days after his last previous home run, Reggie had risen to the occasion once again.

However, he slowed down his pace after that.

The Yankee pace at the start of the season was slow, too. It wasn't too bad, but it suffered from comparison to Boston's. Jim Rice practically tore the league apart with his power hitting. After 50 games, he had 18 home runs and 50 runs batted in. He powered the Red Sox to the top. At the end of May, they had a 34–16 record and a three-game lead over the Yankees, who were 29–17. Steinbrenner was beginning to grow uneasy. Rumors spread early in June that he was considering replacing Martin.

Reggie stuck up for Billy: "Billy Martin isn't the reason we're playing bad. We're not even playing bad so much as the Red Sox are playing good. We don't need a rah-rah manager. We need a manager who knows the game, which Billy does as well as anyone. We're professionals and we know how to play the game.

"There's a lot of time left and we've got a lot of

winning to do and they've got a lot of losing to do. And I've got a lot of home runs to hit," he concluded. And he went out and hit two to help Guidry win his ninth game without a defeat. The skinny, hard-throwing Guidry was as much a sensation as Rice.

But by mid-June, Boston had won 30 of its last 40 games and had pulled six games in front of the Yankees. Reggie went on a tear and reached base 12 straight times at one point, but the Yankees were riddled by injuries, short of pitching, and struggling to stay within reach of the Red Sox.

When the Yankees moved into Fenway Park for their first series of the season with the Red Sox, Boston had a 45–20 record and was running away with the race.

In the Monday night opener, the Red Sox broke a 4–4 tie with a 6-run rally in the eighth inning to embarrass the Yankees, 10–4. More than 32,000 fans packed into the tiny ballpark roared their approval. Reggie made two misplays in the outfield during the rally and made Martin angry.

The next night, Jackson hit his 11th home run and drove in three runs, and little-used shortstop Fred Stanley hit a grand slam home run as the Yankees reversed the rout on the Red Sox, 10–4. However, on the final night of the series the Red Sox ripped the Yankees, 9–2, and the New Yorkers left town eight games back, battling Baltimore and Milwaukee for second place.

Ron Guidry required four days' rest between starts and since his turn had not come up, Martin had not used his ace in this series. Steinbrenner was unhappy about this. He was unhappy about a lot of things.

He talked to Lee MacPhail, president of the American League, who suggested that he talk to the White Sox about trading Martin for Bob Lemon. White Sox owner Bill Veeck was willing, but Steinbrenner didn't want to get involved in such an unusual deal.

So Veeck fired Lemon, 1977 American League "Manager of the Year," and hired black coach Larry Doby in an obvious move to stimulate interest in his team. Lemon had done a good job with the team, but Doby was needed to bring in black fans.

Steinbrenner then wanted to fire Martin and hire Lemon, another former Cleveland Indian, another favorite of Steinbrenner's, and a former pitching coach of the Yankees, but his right-hand man, Rosen, talked him out of it. Rosen contended that Martin was a favorite of the fans in New York and did not deserve to be fired.

Hearing the rumors, Martin asked, "How can you take over a club, win a pennant in your first year, win a World Series in your second year, and be fired in your third year with more than half the year to go? There are men who have been managing fifteen years and never finished higher than fourth, who aren't fired, yet every time I turn around I hear I'm being fired."

Steinbrenner said, "I won't put up with this much longer." But he met with Martin for more than two hours and afterwards announced, "Martin will manage the Yankees for the rest of this season at least, and probably longer. That's final and definite."

Or, so he said.

The double-play combination of Randolph and Dent was in and out of the lineup with injuries. Center-fielder Rivers was in and out of the lineup with leg injuries. He was a runner who couldn't run. Thurman Munson was playing with leg and arm injuries. He was a catcher who couldn't throw. Defensive strength down the middle, considered critical in baseball, had become a sore spot with the Yankees.

Steinbrenner wanted Munson moved into the outfield, but had not provided Martin with a capable catcher to substitute. Half his starting pitchers were struggling with arm miseries. It was all Martin could do to keep his club from falling from sight. "I'm not a quitter," he snarled.

Reggie ripped a home run to touch off a four-run rally in the ninth inning to defeat Detroit, 4–2. Guidry tied the Yankees record with his 12th straight victory at the start of a season. And he was ready when the Red Sox came to Yankee Stadium for a three-game series late in June.

Boston knocked him out, but the Yankees went on to win, 6–4, on Nettles' home run in the 14th inning. Reggie had singled in the tying run in the eighth, but

was out trying to score the winning run from second on a single in the 11th. The Red Sox took the next two to pull 10 games in front of the Yankees, who seemed to be fading fast.

After Reggie went hitless in a doubleheader defeat to Milwaukee, Steinbrenner publicly criticized Jackson. "He's not performing the way he should," the owner said. Jackson said, "I'm doing my best." And went out and hit a grand-slam home run and two singles to put Detroit to rout, 10–2.

Early in July, Guidry set a new team record with his 13th straight triumph since the season's start. However, he fell two short of the major league record as he lost his next start, 6–0, to Milwaukee, which was only his second defeat in his last 25 decisions.

Reggie was slumping. Dropped into the designated hitter slot, he threw his glove against a wall. "I don't need that any longer," he said. Dropped to sixth in the batting order, he took one look at the lineup taped on the dugout wall and took himself out of the lineup, pleading sickness, and returned to the dressing room.

Martin was angered, but didn't do anything about it. Asked about Martin, Reggie said, "I can't be concerned. I'm not for management. I'm not against management. I have enough to do doing my job. Every time I get out there it gets tougher. I thought it would

Wincing with pain, Reggie Jackson goes down after twisting hip with typically hard swing during often painful 1978 season with the New York Yankees. *(Wide World Photos)*

be better this season, but it's just as bad. I'll be glad when it's over with."

At the All-Star Game break on the 11th of July, the traditional mid-season mark, Boston led the Eastern Division of the American League with a 57–26 record. Milwaukee was nine back at 48–35, the Yankees were 11½ back at 46–38, and Baltimore was 13 behind at 45–40. Everyone was conceding the pennant to the Red Sox.

Pleading injury, Reggie removed himself from the All-Star roster, took the break to rest, and got into a hassle with a lady who demanded his autograph during the showing of a movie in a darkened New York theater. "People just won't leave me alone," he sighed.

During the All-Star break, a New York writer reported that Billy Martin was drinking heavily and was troubled by a liver problem. Martin angrily denied it, saying, "I don't drink anything but a few beers and my health is fine. I thought I was talking to that writer in confidence, anyway."

After the All-Star break, Steinbrenner held a closed-door clubhouse meeting with the Yankees. He told them he was dissatisfied with their performance and demanded that they show immediate improvement. In front of them, he rapped Reggie.

Later, Reggie said, "I've been doing what I've been doing for a lot of years. I have 13 home runs and 49 runs batted in. I usually finish fast through the stretch and if I do I'll wind up with close to 30 home runs and 100 RBIs, which is about average for me."

It was and he would.

"If that's not good enough for them, they've got the wrong guy here," Reggie added. "I guess it was my mistake to hit all those home runs in the World Series. Now they expect me to make miracles all the time. I think it is wrong of the man to blame me because we're not playing as well as the other team. What the man did to me, you do to kids. I don't embarrass him by jumping on him when he makes mistakes. And he makes mistakes. If Billy Martin has a bad day managing, I'm not going to say he should be fired. But, sure as anything, the man will fire him. He has to find someone to blame. But if we win, he takes the credit. Well, it's his house. What he tells us to do, we do. In my house, I'm the boss. Here, he's the boss."

Steinbrenner met privately with Martin and asked him to resign, using his failing health as an excuse. Martin refused. So, Steinbrenner told Martin to move Munson into the outfield, move Mike Heath behind the plate, move Gary Thomasson into the outfield, and stick to Jackson as designated hitter.

Martin made the moves he was ordered to make.

On the 17th of July, losers of nine of their last 11 games, having fallen 12 games behind Boston, the Yankees were playing Kansas City at Yankee Stadium.

In the 10th inning of this Monday night game, Jackson came to bat with a man on first.

The power-hitter, Reggie, was seldom asked to sacrifice, but this time Martin flashed the bunt sign to third-base coach Dick Howser, who relayed it to Reggie. Jackson tried to bunt, but fouled the ball back.

Martin decided to let him hit away and flashed this sign to Howser. But Reggie bunted again, fouling it off again. Howser rushed in to confer with Reggie, who said he had missed the sign. "Well, Billy says to hit away," Howser said. Reggie said, "I want to bunt."

He went back to bat and bunted again. Foul again. This time he was out, because a foul bunt for a third strike is an out. This is why even the best bunters seldom try to bunt on what might be a third strike. Martin was angry, as Reggie knew he would be.

Reggie returned to the dugout, took off his glasses, set them on the bench, sat down, and waited for Billy. But, Billy, who said later he was as mad as he ever had been in his life, controlled his temper for fear of a scene such as the previous season's, which might cost him his job, and sent coach Gene Michael to tell Reggie that he was out of the game.

After the Royals went on to win in the 11th inning, Martin went into his office in the clubhouse in a rage, smashed a soft-drink bottle against a wall and threw a clock radio into the hall. He then sent word to Reggie to tell him he was suspended indefinitely. He hinted Reggie might never play for him again.

However, after meeting with Steinbrenner, Rosen, and Cedric Tallis, another aide, Martin reduced the suspension to five days. And didn't seem at all happy about it. He said, "I don't know why Reggie did it, but I'm the manager and I can't have it."

Leaving for his home in California, Reggie said, "He doesn't want me around here; he should be happy now. The man hasn't talked to me for a long time; why should he talk to me now, even to tell me what he thought of me?"

Reggie knew he had done wrong. He had acted, as he so often did, impulsively: "I wasn't hitting good. I told Thurman Munson I was going to bunt before I even got up and got the first bunt sign. I wanted to move the man along. I wanted to help the hitter behind me get the winning run in. I guarantee you, if I get a good sacrifice bunt down, I'm a hero. I didn't, so I'm a bum."

One recalled Reggie once saying, "Baseball is not all hitting home runs and tipping your cap to a cheering crowd. It's striking out, too. Or fumbling the play. It's trying too hard and making a mistake and getting fined for it and booed for it."

He was wrong for bunting against orders, but truly believed that if he had succeeded in sacrificing successfully he would have been hailed as a hero.

He was fined. His suspension cost him about $10,000 in salary. And when he returned, he was booed. Billy Martin had many more fans in New York than Reggie did.

To New Yorkers, Martin was street-tough, a fighter, a little guy who battled the big guys. To them, he was a hero. And Jackson was just an overpaid player.

While Reggie was suspended, Martin's Yankees hit the low point of what would develop into a historic campaign. After the games of the 19th of July, Boston had a 62–28 record and a 14-game lead over the New Yorkers, who were 48–42.

For the record, no team ever had come from that far back that late in the season to win. The Miracle Braves of 1914 fell farther back, 15 games, but on July 4th, and within the next two weeks crept a lot closer. The Giants of 1951 came from 13½ games back on August 12th, which remains the latest surge, but they never fell 14 back. The 1973 Mets came from 12 back on the 4th of July.

These were all National League teams. The only American League club to come from as far back as 6½ games back on the 4th of July was the 1907 Detroit Tigers. The Yankees were 11½ back on the 4th of July and 14 games on the 19th of July, and no one, absolutely no one, gave them any chance at all.

They were a team in turmoil. The five-game deficit they had overcome the year before could not be compared to this one, though their troubles were comparable. And now their star was on suspension and their manager was staggering.

When Reggie returned to the team in Chicago, he was asked if he was sorry. He said, "I'm sorry I didn't swing away and strike out so I could have avoided this hassle. I was just trying to help the team."

When his comments were relayed to Martin, Billy, who had demanded an apology, snarled, "If he doesn't shut his mouth, he won't play. And I don't care what Steinbrenner says. He can replace me right now if he doesn't like it."

Martin had been on edge for a long time, acting angry and speaking profanely. At the airport he told several writers, "Those two guys [Jackson and Steinbrenner] deserve each other. One's a liar and one's convicted."

The latter referred to the owner's conviction for having concealed campaign contributions.

Asked if he was speaking off the record, Martin snapped, "No, that's on the record. Report it." The writers did.

Reading the statements, Steinbrenner was shocked. "I can't believe Billy would make statements like that if he hadn't been drinking. I don't know if that's an excuse. I don't know what I'm going to do."

In New York, Martin denied making the statements.

But the following day, on the 24th of July, Steinbrenner asked for his resignation and Martin gave it to him. In a public press conference Martin announced he had not been fired, but was resigning for the good of the team. He said he was sorry he had said the things he had. He broke down in tears and could not finish his statement. He left, looking like a sick man. Rosen said, "He is a sick man." Martin admitted he had a liver problem and said he was reducing his drinking.

Bob Lemon immediately was named to succeed him.

Steinbrenner took a lot of heat. New York fans, fond of Martin, booed the boss and his new manager. Newspaper columns were full of criticism of the owner. Rosen advised Steinbrenner that he was in danger of losing the town's support.

Five days after firing Martin, at an afternoon Old-Timer's Game preceding the regular game at Yankee Stadium, Martin was introduced with the dramatic public address announcement that he would return to the managerial role in 1980, with Lemon becoming general manager.

No one in the know believed it. The inside opinion was that Steinbrenner had bought a little time by making Martin happy and a year and a half later maybe no one would want Martin to return.

Martin received a standing ovation and strutted off. Within a few weeks he called a press conference to announce that his health was fine, his drinking moderate, and he was ready to return as manager at any time. He blamed Reggie for all his problems.

Steinbrenner said, "Under the circumstances I can't

Reggie tells reporters his side of the story after being benched in Monday night, July 18, 1978, game with Kansas City for striking out on a bunt attempt after having been ordered by Billy Martin to "hit away." Reggie was suspended, Martin was fired, and Yankees fell far out of the race before rallying.

(Wide World Photos)

believe he'd say these things, go out of his way to say them. I don't know what I can say."

What could he say? Essentially, Martin had called Steinbrenner and Jackson liars. Yet it was Martin who denied he had a health problem, then admitted it, then denied it. It was Martin who denied he had a drinking problem, then admitted it, then denied it. It was Martin who made the statement, then denied it, then admitted it.

"What can I say?" asked Reggie. "I don't want to kick a man when he's down. It's obvious we didn't get along. Maybe it was my fault. Maybe some of it was his. But I don't believe I should be blamed for all of his troubles or all the team's troubles. I don't believe he should be blamed for all the team's troubles. I didn't fire him. I wouldn't have.

"I don't want to say too much. No one wants to hear the truth. I have a bad reputation now and it will haunt me as long as I stay in the game, no matter where I go, no matter what I do. I have proven myself as a player, but not as a person. I have made mistakes. Who hasn't? I don't mean to do anyone wrong.

"I'd just like to play baseball and do the best I can and enjoy the game, but a lot of the fun has been gone out of it for a long time now. There are other things in life besides baseball. Maybe when I stop playing, I can be forgotten and I can start to live again."

The Comeback Kings

The fellow who once wanted to be remembered forever now asked only to be forgotten. The pressure of his profession showed on him. He seemed worn out, tired. The controversies had sapped a lot of the spirit from him. But he was still a pro, still a player, and he was going to go on playing to a happier ending than anyone ever expected at that time.

At the time Martin was fired, the Yankees had a 44–40 record, but had won five straight games and were 10½ games behind Boston. Lemon was 57 years old and an experienced manager. He had been hired and he had been fired before. He had never managed a title team, but had done a good job with bad teams. After being fired by the White Sox, he had gone to his home in Long Beach. Called by Steinbrenner, he accepted the Yankee job. Within one month he was back in the big leagues.

A tough fellow, he was soft-spoken but firm. When he was unhappy with any of the Yankees, he told them so, but he told them in private and he did not rant and rave and threaten to throw punches.

He calmed the team down and restored order to it. He proved he was no puppet manager by moving Munson back behind the plate and benching Thomasson. He retained Reggie as his designated hitter, but Reggie accepted this. "From him, it's not so hard to take," he said.

The players liked Lemon and responded positively to his style. Ed Figueroa went to him to complain he hadn't been pitched enough. Lemon returned the pitcher to the regular rotation and he started to win consistently. Lemon returned Catfish Hunter to the rotation and Hunter started to win consistently. Guidry was still going good. The pitching started to straighten out. The hitters, such as Jackson and Munson, started to hit with consistency and produce power and runs.

Rusty, Reggie didn't actually return to the lineup until ten days after he had been suspended. With the spotlight shining on him, he had a home run, four singles, and four runs batted in during a double-header with Cleveland. He went on a tear in which he hit .545 for a week. Clearly, he was ready to carry the club for a while.

After Martin was removed and before Lemon arrived, Dick Howser managed the club for one game, which the Yankees lost to end their five-game winning streak. On the morning of July 25th, as Lemon took over, here were the divisional standings:

July 25	W L	GB
BOSTON	63–33	
MILWAUKEE	57–38	5½
BALTIMORE	54–43	9½
NEW YORK	52–43	10½

The Comeback Kings

The Yankees were in fourth place, not only 10½ games behind Boston, but with Milwaukee and Baltimore between them.

Guidry pitched a shutout for his major-league-leading 15th victory as the Yankees clipped Kansas City, 4–0, in the first game of Lemon's managerial regime. They won two more to make it eight wins in the team's last nine games before they lost again.

The Yankees then divided a four-game series with Minnesota and took two straight from Texas. In the same spell of time—from the 25th of July to the 1st of August—while the Yankees lost only three games out of ten, Boston lost four straight and six out of eight.

Boston had, in fact, lost 11 out of their last 15 games, while the Yankees had lost only four out of 16, thus swiftly slicing 7½ games from the Red Sox lead over the New Yorkers. Rice hadn't been hitting and the Red Sox hadn't been winning and as the Red Sox moved into Yankee Stadium for a two-game series on August 2nd, here is how their lead had shrunk:

July 19	W L	GB
BOSTON	62–28	
MILWAUKEE	53–37	−9
BALTIMORE	51–42	−12½
NEW YORK	48–42	−14

August 1	W L	GB
BOSTON	66–39	
MILWAUKEE	60–44	–5½
NEW YORK	60–46	–6½
BALTIMORE	58–47	–8

Yet the Yankees blew a golden opportunity and the flame of hope flickered out again.

With more than 50,000 fans screaming, the Yankees surged to a 5–0 lead in the first three innings of the first game. But the Red Sox rallied with four runs in the next three innings and tied it with the help of a double by Rice in the eighth inning.

After two rain delays, the game was still tied after 14 innings when it was postponed to completion the following night. Then, Evans, Hobson, Burleson, and Rice ripped singles to provide the Red Sox with the winning runs in a 7–5 game in the third inning of the night and 17 of the game.

Another crowd of more than 50,000 was on hand and the Red Sox won the following game, the regularly scheduled game, also, 8–1, with the help of two-run home runs by Fred Lynn and Rice. Lynn's was the first he ever had hit in Yankee Stadium, while Rice's was only his second in 33 games.

The Red Sox seemed to have saved themselves and shoved the Yankees back into fourth place, 8½ games back.

The Comeback Kings

The feeling was that the Red Sox had straightened out in time, had delivered a knockout punch to the Yankees, and were not apt to be caught by Milwaukee or Baltimore either. Manager Don Zimmer's Bostonians breathed easier.

However, this Yankee club had demonstrated it was a tough team. "Few of us thought we had much chance," admitted Jackson, "but we weren't going to give up without trying." They put together six- and seven-game winning streaks during the rest of the month and wound up 19–8 for the month. Meanwhile Boston, back on the beam, went 19–10 and had its lead over New York cut only a little, back to 6½ games at the end of August.

Entering the final month of the season, New York and Boston had discouraged Baltimore and Milwaukee in several series and those two were slipping out of the race.

The first week in September, New York won five out of seven, while Boston won only two out of six. Boston was in trouble again as the two teams went into two crucial series, head to head, only four games apart.

Boston had been almost unbeatable in its home park, but the Yankees slammed 21 hits around Fenway Park to rout the Red Sox in the first of the four-game set, 15–3. Munson, White, and Randolph had three hits each and Randolph drove in five runs as the Yankees clobbered their ex-ace Torrez. Hunter, who had been hot lately, didn't last long, but young Ken Clay mopped up effectively.

Boston's lead was down to three games and the Red Sox were running scared.

The Red Sox made seven errors and the Yankees made 17 hits as Boston was blasted, 13–2, in the second game. Rivers and Piniella had three hits each and Jackson clouted a three-run homer. Young Jim Beattie held Boston scoreless until the ninth. The Yankees now were talking about another title as they raced into their dressing room.

Boston's lead was down to two games.

The Red Sox were embarrassed in the Saturday afternoon, nationally televised third game, 7–0. Rivers and Dent drove in two runs each and Guidry became the first left-hander to shut out Boston in its tiny ballpark in four years.

Boston's lead was one game and the dejection of the Red Sox was written in their glum expressions.

Gaining confidence with each game, the Yankees slashed 18 more hits and cut up their hosts, 7–4, in Sunday afternoon's fourth game to sweep the series here where the Red Sox seldom lost. Munson, White, and Dent had three hits each. Figueroa, another hot hurler in the second half, went six innings, and Gossage wrapped it up.

Boston had been tied, with 20 games to go. The Red Sox had lost a 14-game lead in eight weeks.

The Comeback Kings

The Yankees had outhit the Red Sox, 67–21, and outscored them, 42–9, in the four games.

The Red Sox made 12 errors, collapsing under the pressure of the Yankee drive.

Lemon said, "A sweep was more than I could have asked for." Jackson said, "It's in our hands now."

A depressed Don Zimmer said, "We're not finished yet." Rice said, "We have to fight back."

Rice hit two home runs as the Red Sox beat Baltimore, 5–4, to regain first place the following night as the Yankees were idle. However, Boston then lost their next three straight while the Yankees won two out of three from Detroit to move 1½ games in front as the two squared off in their second series.

Guidry threw his second straight two-hit shutout at Boston as the Yankees defeated the Red Sox, 4–0, in the Friday night opener of the three-game series before 54,901 frenzied fans in Yankee Stadium. Chambliss and Nettles hit back-to-back home runs to pace the attack. And the Yankees were 2½ games in the lead.

For the first time in the last six meetings, the Red Sox broke in front, 2–0, on Rice's two-run homer in Saturday afternoon's nationally televised contest before 55,091 fans in the Stadium. But Jackson singled in one run, then hit a home run to tie it. Hunter and Torrez were locked in the tie until the last of the ninth when Rivers tripled and scored as Rice fell down catching a fly ball by Munson. The Yankee lead was 3½ games.

The Red Sox had lost five straight games and had lost six in a row to the Yankees over two weekends when they bounced back to beat the New Yorkers, 7–3, before 55,088 fans on Sunday afternoon. With this, they moved back to within 2½ games of the lead they had held so long. Yastrzemski, the old pro, singled in one run and homered for another. George Scott, hitless in 36 at-bats, doubled in another run. Beattie was beaten as Dennis Eckersley and reliever Bob Stanley stopped the Yankees.

However, here is how the divisional lead changed hands over the ten-day period, which included the two crucial series:

Sept. 6	W L	GB
BOSTON	86–52	
NEW YORK	82–56	−4

Sept. 17	W L	GB
NEW YORK	90–58	
BOSTON	88–61	−2½

The Yankees were jubilant, but Lemon cautioned, "There's still a lot of time left." The Red Sox were depressed, but Zimmer warned, "It's not over yet."

It wasn't.

The Comeback Kings

Suffering from a let-down, the Yankees lost four of their next seven games. Suddenly they could see what had been so hard to win slipping easily from their grasp. However, the Red Sox lost three out of seven and gained only a half game.

The Yankees split two with Milwaukee, while Boston took two from Detroit. In Toronto, the Yankees were shocked as Guidry was bombed by the Blue Jays and beaten, 8–1, in the opener of a doubleheader. He had won seven straight and 22 out of 25 and had not been hit hard in 2½ months.

However, the Yankees came back to rally for three runs in the ninth inning of the nightcap to pull out a vital victory, 3–2. Singles by Randolph, Piniella, Chambliss, and Nettles saved the New Yorkers. Meanwhile, Torrez lost his sixth straight as the Red Sox lost a single game to Detroit, 12–2, and dropped two games back with 10 games to go.

Jackson crashed a two-run double to get the Yankees going to a 7–2 triumph over Toronto as Hunter and Gossage combined to beat the Blue Jays. The Red Sox topped the Tigers, 5–1. The next night the Red Sox took a 4–3 lead into the last of the ninth, but blew it and lost to Detroit 5–4. But the Yankees blew one, too, 8–7, in 10 innings in Cleveland.

On Saturday afternoon in Cleveland, the Indians bombed Beattie and the Yankees, 10–1. Meanwhile, Rice hit his 43rd home run as the Red Sox and Luis

Tiant trimmed Toronto, 3–1, to move within one game of the top spot. Rice now had 387 total bases, the most by any American Leaguer since Jimmy Foxx had 398 in 1938. Soon he would become the first major leaguer since Henry Aaron in 1959 to reach 400.

The Red Sox had risen to the top on their power hitting, started to slip when Rice slumped, and fell from the lead when their hitting fell off drastically. But Rice had begun to bomb the ball again and Boston was battling back. It was said they "choked" when they slumped from 14 in front and lost seven straight and the lead to the Yankees. Perhaps they did, but this slur is difficult to live with and it is to their credit that they came on again and demonstrated strength of character under dreadful pressure through the final weeks.

On Sunday, Guidry gave the Yankees a 4–0 triumph over Cleveland, while Boston scrambled to a 7–6 victory over Toronto. Both sides were off Monday as they entered the last week of the season one game apart with six games to go. The tension was terrific. The players were performing under great pressure. Both teams won and won until the last day.

On Tuesday night, Dent and Rivers supported Figueroa with run-scoring doubles as the Yankees defeated visiting Toronto, 4–1, while Eckersley blanked Detroit, 6–0, for Boston with Rice ramming a two-run home run. On Wednesday night, Jackson and

Nettles helped Hunter to his ninth win in the last 10 decisions, 5–1, over Toronto, while hot-hitting Carlton Fisk helped Tiant and Boston to a 5–2 victory over Toronto.

"I've been in five pennant races, and this is the first tough one. It should be fun, but I'm not enjoying it," confessed Reggie.

On Thursday night, Guidry ran his record to 24–3 and his strikeouts to a Yankee record 243 as he four-hit Toronto, 3–1. But Boston stayed close on Jim Rice's 43rd home run and Torrez's three-hitter over Detroit, 1–0. On Friday night, Munson, Jackson, and Piniella hit successive run-scoring singles in the eighth inning as the Yankees rallied to pull out a 3–1 triumph over Cleveland behind Beattie and Gossage, but Boston hung on as Lynn drove in five runs to lead an 11–0 romp over Toronto.

On Saturday afternoon, Ed Figueroa won his eighth straight decision and became a 20-game winner for the first time in his career as Jackson's 27th homer of the season helped defeat Cleveland, 7–0. Dennis Eckersley took his 20th victory as Boston took Toronto, 5–1, but at this point they were left with little hope that they would win and the Yankees lose on Sunday to tie.

"All we can do is hope," Zimmer sighed.

Hope paid off on that first of October afternoon as the rallying Red Sox won their eighth straight game,

5–0, on Tiant's two-hitter against Toronto, while Hunter was hammered from the box by a barrage of home runs and Cleveland stunned the Yankees, 9–2, to end the Yankees' six-game winning streak. After 162 games, the two bitter rivals were even at 99–63.

The coin flip to decide the site of a playoff had been won by Boston and a deeply disappointed Yankee team took off for Fenway Park to meet the rejuvenated Red Sox on national television on Monday afternoon. Hot again, having battled back, having the home-field advantage, the Red Sox were favored to provide an unhappy ending to the Yankees' Cinderella story.

"Well, I guess this is the way it was meant to be— one game between two great teams to settle it all," sighed Jackson. Rice said, "It is tough to play six months and have it settled on one day." Boston shortstop Dyrol Burleson spoke for all when he said, "This is the biggest day of our lives."

On the big day, the Yankees turned to a weary Guidry, working with only three days' rest instead of his usual four, while the Red Sox went with the ex-Yankee, Torrez.

Torrez was tough for six innings as Boston took a 2–0 lead on a home run by Yastrzemski and a run-scoring single by Rice. The packed park of 32,295 fans went wild. But this is a come-from-behind Yankee team. With one out in the seventh, Chambliss and

The Comeback Kings

White singled. With two out, Dent lifted a fly ball that just cleared and landed in the screen atop the famous Fenway Park "Green Monster," that close-in wall in left field. Dent, a low-average hitter who had hit only four home runs all year, always was a good clutch-hitter, and his three-run home run gave the Yankees the lead.

After Rivers walked, Torrez was taken out and

Reggie runs by owner George Steinbrenner's box to slap palms with joyous boss following Jackson's home run in the eighth inning that proved the winning run in Yankees' 5–4 win over Red Sox at Boston in one-game playoff, Monday, October 2, 1978, to part tie between the two teams for the title in the American League East. Front office official Al Rosen stands between two, while Thurman Munson and Paul Blair (2) look on from dugout. *(Wide World Photos)*

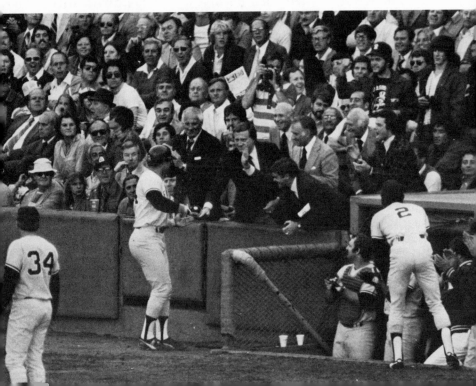

Stanley brought in. Rivers stole second and raced home on Munson's double to make it 4–2. The following inning, Jackson clouted a clutch home run to make it 5–2. As it turned out, his side needed it.

The Red Sox rallied for two runs off reliever Gossage to make it 5–4 in the last of the eighth on a double by Jerry Remy and singles by Yastrzemski, Fisk, and Lynn. Lemon stayed with Gossage and he got out of the jam.

And he stayed with him in the last of the ninth as the Red Sox threatened again. With one out, Burleson walked. Remy looped a single to right. Piniella lost sight of it or he might have caught it. As it was, he saw it just in time to stab it with his glove as it was about to bounce past him. That saved a tying run, though it still left men on first and second with Rice and Yastrzemski coming up.

The excitement was enormous. Gossage fired fastballs. Rice got too far under one and lifted a fly-out to right. Two out. Yaz got under another and lifted a foul ball off third base and Nettles caught it. Three out!

The Yankees were the winners and raced to hug one another and run off together in triumph, while the Red Sox sat in the dugout as though in disbelief, deeply depressed now that it was all over.

Champagne popped in celebration in the Yankee dressing room while the Red Sox still sat in their dugout. Zimmer's head was down. Rice's head was down.

Yastrzemski had tears in his eyes as he faced the press and said, "It seems such a shame that in the end we lose it in one game. There should be no loser. But I guess there had to be."

In the Yankee dressing room, Jackson, whose home run had turned out to be the winning run, which won the championship for his side, said, "I'm proud to have hit it, but the big home run was Bucky's. That was the one that turned this game around, so give the credit for the victory to Dent.

"We're winners, but they're not losers. It's the thrill of a lifetime to win, but I'm sorry they lost. They're as good as we are. Another game, another day, maybe they win. Anyone who says they choked doesn't know what he's talking about and didn't see them this last week."

But a comparison of the standings from the low points of the Yankee season, 14 games behind, to the finish, one game in front, tells the story.

				INTERIM RECORD	
July 19	W L	GB			W L
Boston	62–28		Boston		37–36
New York	48–42	−14	New York		52–21

Oct. 2	W L	GB
New York	100–63	
Boston	99–64	−1

The Yankees wound up with the best record in baseball. Actually, the Red Sox wound up with the second-best record, better than the 92–70 with which Kansas City won the American League West, or the 95–67 with which Los Angeles won the National League East, or the 90–72 with which Philadelphia won the National League West. But Boston did not make the playoffs.

For that matter, Milwaukee, finishing third, 6½ games behind New York with a 93–69 mark, had a better record than two other divisional titlists, and Baltimore, finishing fourth, nine games back with a 90–71 mark, had a better record than one other. Clearly the American League East was the toughest division of all, which makes the Yankee victory all the more meaningful.

And no team in the history of the major leagues ever came from so far back so late in the season as the Yankees of 1978. Some saw this as a tribute to Bob Lemon, whose record running the team was 55–22 compared to Martin's 54–40. For this, Lemon would be named "Manager of the Year" in the league for the second straight year. "Fired in June, hired in July, and a champion in October," Lemon sighed. "It's absolutely unbelievable."

Munson said, "He settled us down. He took charge. He didn't create controversy. He freed us to play ball, Martin can manage, but Lemon was what we needed this season."

At the dugout, Reggie reaches for hand of jacketed N.Y. manager Bob Lemon, who took over for Billy Martin in midseason and led Yankees to the top. Hollering his happiness for the homer that sealed the playoff victory over the Red Sox is Thurman Munson at left, while Lou Piniella is next to Munson. *(Wide World Photos)*

Jackson was asked if the Yankees could have won with Martin. "No way," he said. "I don't want to put the knock on Billy. We won with him, too. But we would never have won this one with him. And the way we won it makes it mean all the more."

Under Lemon, Reggie had responded to pressure as usual, driving in 35 runs in the last 37 games. This was similar to his spectacular stretch run the year before. Despite missing 14 games, which cost him the kind of totals he usually produced, Reggie, averaging .274, hit 27 home runs and drove in 97 runs. He struck out 133 times to stretch his major league mark in this department, but also drove in his 1,000th run during the campaign and became one of the few men ever to hit 20 home runs or more more than ten seasons in succession.

At .314, Piniella was the only .300 hitter on the team. Munson missed at .297. No one hit 30 home runs. Piniella tied Jackson at 27. No one drove in 100 runs. Nettles with 93 and Chambliss with 90 trailed Reggie. But like his old A's, Reggie's new Yankees got the key hits when they counted.

They benefitted from superb pitching by Guidry at 25–3, Figueroa at 20–9, Hunter at 12–6, and Gossage with 10 victories and 27 saves. Gossage had 11 losses, but a fine 2.01 earned-run average. Guidry's 1.74 ERA was the best by a left-handed pitcher since Carl Hubbell's 1.66 in the National League forty years earlier.

Guidry would win the Cy Young Award. Many thought he should win the Most Valuable Player Award, but that went to Rice, the Red Sox slugger who led the major leagues with 46 home runs and 139 runs batted in. Reggie could not be compared to Rice statistically this season.

Yet it was a month-long slump by Rice that led to the Red Sox downfall and it was a month-long surge by Reggie at the finish that once again led the Yankees to the top. And with the playoffs and possibly the World Series ahead of him, Reggie again was in his element and the leader of his side.

9

Coming Through

Following their climactic victory in Boston, the Yankees had to fly to Kansas City to open the 1978 American League pennant playoffs against the Western Division winners, the Royals, the next night.

Some feared this would be anticlimactic for the Yanks, that they would be worn out. They had to open the series with two games in Kansas City and would not be able to use a weary Guidry until later. They had beaten the Royals two straight seasons in playoffs that were settled in the last inning of the last game and this could be Kansas City's turn.

Coming Through

Naturally, the Yankees went right out in the opener and ripped the Royals, 7–1, collecting 16 hits off 21-game winner Dennis Leonard and his successors while rookie Jim Beattie limited the Royals to two hits.

Reggie reached base every time he came up. He had two walks, a single, and a double, and when reliever Al Hrabosky went into his "Mad Hungarian" act, storming around the mound and scowling at the hitter, Reggie ripped him for a three-run home run. That gave Reggie five home runs and nine runs batted in in his last two post-season games.

Kansas City did come back to win the second game, 7–1, to even the series as Figueroa was knocked out in one inning and Larry Gura subdued the Yankees. Reggie walked his first time up—making it twelve straight times he had reached base in post-season play —and later singled and scored a run, but this was not the New Yorker's night. The team headed home to Yankee Stadium.

George Brett matched Jackson run for run in the thrilling third game. A master batsman, Brett homered in the first inning. Reggie homered to tie the game, 1–1, in the second. Brett homered again in the third, but Munson doubled and Reggie singled him in to tie it up again, then Munson scored on a wild throw by shortstop Patek to make it 3–2 in the fourth. Brett hit his third straight home run to tie it in the fifth, but White and Munson singled and Jackson hit a sacrifice fly to put the Yankees in front again, 4–3, in the sixth.

Hunter had been hit hard, Gossage took over, and the Royals took the lead in the eighth. Amos Otis doubled and Darrell Porter and Clint Hurdle singled in the rally which put the Royals in front, 5–4, in this pivotal game. But then, in the home half, White singled and Munson, suffering from a sore shoulder, hit his first home run in 55 games to win it for the Yankees, 6–5, in front of 55,000 cheering customers.

Jackson had hit in his seventh straight post-season game. He was batting better than .500 in this playoff at 14-for-27. And he had set a record for playoffs with his 15th RBI. But he said afterward, "Give the credit to Munson. He hit the home run that won it. And feel for Brett. Like I hit three straight home runs in a World Series game, he hit three straight in a play-off, but he won't get the credit I did because my team won and his team lost."

A subdued Brett said, "Maybe later they'll mean more, but right now my home runs don't mean much because they didn't win the game for us and if we lose one more game we've lost one more playoff."

They lost one more game and they lost one more playoff, their third straight to the Yankees. It was 2–1 and a four-hitter by Leonard was a loser. Home runs by Nettles in the second and by White in the sixth produced all the runs the Yankees needed.

Guidry, acting tired, struggled through eight innings, scattering seven hits, for his 26th victory of the season, before Gossage wrapped it up for him.

Coming Through

Willie Wilson singled and scored the Royals' only run in the fifth. Frank White hit a one-out single in the seventh, but Patek's line drive, which looked as if it were headed into left field for a game-tying double, was snared by the brilliant third baseman, Nettles, and he turned it into an inning-ending double play.

Otis opened the ninth with a double, but Gossage blew down the last three Royals to end it as the Yankees went into their victory dance.

It was the 32nd American League pennant for this greatest of franchises, the first for manager Bob Lemon, and the first for any American League manager to take over a team at mid-season. Two National League managers—Charlie Grimm in 1932 and Gabby Hartnett in 1938, both with the Cubs—had done it before, but neither went on to win the World Series, which now was within Lemon's reach. If he had not already been vindicated for making the controversial managerial change in mid-season, Steinbrenner now was. The owner embraced his manager, who said, "I can't believe this is happening."

"This season, this team, every season with this team is unbelievable," agreed Reggie Jackson, whose teams now had won seven divisional laurels and five pennants in his career.

He was voted Most Valuable Player of the playoffs for his .461 batting average, six hits, and six runs batted in. The third MVP award of his post-season career, it re-established him as the game's greatest clutch hitter. "Now all I've got to do is do it again in the World Series."

He would. Incredibly, he would.

The Dodgers had frustrated the Phillies in the National League pennant playoffs, the second straight playoff win for them and the third straight playoff loss for the Phillies, who, like the Royals, were feeling frustrated. The Dodgers felt certain they would turn the tables on the Yankees this time, but as the Royals and Phillies had demonstrated, there is no rule that every team gets its turn. The Phillies had never won a World Series. The Yankees had won 21. And they would make it 22.

The Series opened in Dodger Stadium before crowds of close to 56,000 fans. The Dodgers had set a major league mark with 3.3 million fans in attendance at home, while the Yankees had been happy to draw 2.3 million.

Jim "Junior" Gilliam, a Dodger coach and former player, had died of a stroke just before the Series started. The Dodgers dedicated the Series to his memory and players like Dusty Baker and Davey Lopes spoke constantly of being inspired by him and wanting to win for him.

Baker hit one home run and Lopes hit two off Hunter to help the Dodgers to a 6–0 lead. They went on to coast to an 11–5 triumph behind Tommy John and Terry Forster. Dent drove in two runs.

Jackson wasted two singles and a home run. His home run went 450 feet before it reached the back of the right-field bullpen in the seventh. It was one of the longest in the history of the stadium. When he hit it, Jackson just stood and watched it until it landed.

The first run off John, it ended the pitcher's string of 23 straight scoreless innings. It was Reggie's eighth home run in World Series play and sixth in four consecutive Series games, surpassing the record of five in four straight games by Lou Gehrig in 1928 and 1932.

Told this later, Reggie said, "Hey, thanks for telling me. That's nice. Gehrig was one of the greats of all time. I feel pretty good about being in his company. I'd feel better if we'd won, but we will, you'll see."

They did not win the second game. Reggie doubled off Burt Hooten in the third to drive in two runs and give the Yankees a 2–0 lead. But Ron Cey singled in a run in the fourth and hit a three-run home run in the sixth off Catfish to carry the Dodgers to a 4–2 lead. White singled, Blair doubled, and Reggie grounded in a run to make it 4–3 in the seventh. Reggie had all the runs batted in, but the big moment was just ahead of him.

Nettles, black and blue from two diving catches on the hard Dodger infield, which deprived Baker and Cey of extra-base hits, had kept the Yankees close.

In the ninth, clutch-hitter Dent singled off relief pitcher Forster. White sacrificed him to second. Blair walked. Hard-throwing rookie Bob Welch, brought up at mid-season and termed the iceman by the Dodgers for his pressure performances, got Munson on a liner to right.

The bat appears bent from the force of his swing as Reggie Jackson comes through in the clutch with two-run blow to put the Yankees in front of the Dodgers in the second game of the 1978 World Series in Los Angeles.

(Wide World Photos)

That brought up Jackson with two out and two on. It was a dramatic moment, the veteran against the rookie, a kid challenging the top pressure hitter in the game. Welch threw nothing but fastballs. The first was a swinging strike, a big swing that thrilled the fans. The second was a high, tight one that dropped Reggie into the dirt. The third, fourth, and fifth were fastballs fouled back. The tension was tremendous.

The sixth and seventh pitches were high and outside. Reggie didn't bite and the count was 3-and-2. The eighth pitch was another fastball fouled back. Reggie stepped out, took off his helmet and glasses, wiped away the sweat, then stepped back in. Welch stared in, wound up, and threw. Reggie swung and missed. They stared at each other for a split second as if they couldn't believe it was over. Then the crowd erupted in noise, the Dodgers rushed to embrace their young hero, and Jackson jerked away in frustration and threw his bat into the dugout.

The bat just missed a couple of his teammates, clattering against a wall. As Reggie dove into the dugout, Lemon went to console him and Reggie pushed him away and went down the tunnel to the clubhouse. It was the sort of thing Martin might have made an issue of, but Lemon let it go. "I understand he was upset and I shouldn't have gotten in his way," the manager remarked later.

Reggie calmed down. As he always does, he gave

credit where it was due. "Give the young guy the credit," he said. "He beat me, one on one. He came in with 50 thousand people watching him in the ballpark and 50 million people watching him on television, and he did the job."

The dramatic duel had lasted nine pitches and seven minutes. Experts called it one of the most memorable moments in World Series history. It was a tribute to Jackson that they called it that, and a tribute to Welch that he won it.

Dodger Billy North, Reggie's old sparring partner, said, "It was an incredible confrontation. I looked all around the ballpark and I said to myself, this is what the World Series is all about. This is championship play. This is the thrill of sports at its most exciting."

Dodger manager Tommy Lasorda said, "Sweeping the two here, we have to be favored now." Warned Jackson, "Ours is a team that always comes back."

It was that.

Maybe it needed a little controversy to stir it up. Some said the New York newspaper strike, which had gone on for a long time, had helped the Yankees by keeping any troubles on the team out of print in the Big Town. But, now, with newspaper, radio, and television reporters from across the country covering the fall classic, three incidents attracted attention. There was the Jackson-Lemon bumping bit. Then there was another bumping bit between Rivers and a team official when the outfielder tried to take a friend on the team bus. Finally, it was revealed that Lemon had been voted only a half share of the bonus money.

These shares were not small. Reggie's shares had averaged above $20,000 each of his three winning years with the A's and would be better than $25,000 each of his two years with the Yankees. But with the kind of money Reggie was making, a full share would mean a lot more to Lemon, who was making an estimated $100,000 in salary.

Lemon didn't want to make much of it. "I'm just happy to be here," he said. "Any money I make is gravy." Jackson said, "Whatever we vote the man, it's our business. He knows we appreciate him and he knows we have to give something to Billy Martin, too. We try to be fair. We're paying players who can't play a full share."

The Yankees had several pitchers sidelined. When Willie Randolph was sidelined for the Series, his critical spot at second base was taken by a rookie, Mickey Doyle, who had come up late in the season. The speedster Rivers was limping on a lame leg. Catcher Munson was throwing with a lame arm. Slugger Chambliss had such a sore hand he could hardly grip the bat.

The Dodgers moved into New York with a two-game lead and had to be heavily favored. But the Yankees were the kind of club that overcame all obstacles.

Finally, Friday, for the third game before 56,447 fans in Yankee Stadium, Guidry got in there. You could see he was weary. He was struggling all the way, without his usual fastball. He gave up eight hits and seven walks. He gave up a run on a walk to North and a hit by Bill Russell. He loaded the bases with two out in the fifth and sixth innings and got out of it both times.

Graig Nettles got him out of trouble in the third, fifth, and sixth innings with jumping, diving, twisting glove plays at third. Each time he hit the ground and got up to throw runners out, Lasorda admitted later, "He gave one of the greatest exhibitions I've ever seen in baseball."

He also singled and scored one run. White hit a home run for another. Dent singled and scored a run, Munson driving him in. Jackson singled in another to wrap it up at 5–1. And later, Reggie said, "Nettles has to be the hero. He decided this game and may have turned the entire Series around. Without him, we lose. And he plays like that all the time." Nettles smiled and said, "It's nice to be noticed. It's nicer to win."

Nettles had put the Yankees back into it and on Saturday afternoon they won what turned out to be the big game of the Series to even it up. Another crowd of more than 56,000 turned out to watch Figueroa face John. But Tidrow had to come in to do the job when Figueroa faltered early, and Gossage had to wrap it up.

A three-run home run by Reggie Smith, the only big blow of the Series by that heavy hitter, had given the Dodgers a 3–0 lead. The Yankees had to battle back after a 40-minute delay because of rain.

In the sixth, White beat out a single, Munson walked, and Jackson drove a single to right to score White. He had driven in runs in every game of this Series and eight straight games in World Series play, tying Gehrig's all-time record. This one spoiled John's shutout and set the stage for the most controversial play of the Series.

Lou Piniella hit a low liner to shortstop. Leaning low to his left, Russell seemed to catch the ball, then drop it. He picked it up, ran to second to force out Jackson, then threw to first in an attempt to complete the double play on Piniella.

With the hit, Jackson had started for second. Thinking Russell was going to catch the ball, he started back for first so he couldn't be doubled off base. He was frozen on the base paths, directly in line with the throw, looking at Russell as the shortstop threw.

The throw hit him in the hip and bounced away as Piniella reached first safely and Munson raced home with a run.

Television replays seemed to show Russell deliberately dropping the ball and Jackson deliberately shifting his weight to put his hip in line with the throw. But, if so, both moves were swift and subtle, and the umpire, Frank Pulli, well might not have spotted them. Dodger manager Lasorda raced onto the field to argue angrily that Piniella should have been called out on Jackson's interference. He lost the argument but he was still angry about it after the game and, for that matter, after the Series.

Later, Russell said he did not deliberately drop the line drive. "It hit the heel of my glove and bounced off," he said. He seemed sincere. Reggie said he did not deliberately let himself get hit with the throw. "I'm a slow thinker. I don't think that fast. I don't move that fast. That's why I'm a designated hitter and not a player," he said. He did not seem sincere. He smiled as he spoke.

The first baseman, Garvey, a friend and fan of Jackson's who called him "the best clutch hitter in baseball," said, "There's no doubt he deliberately let himself get hit. But it was smart on his part."

John got out of the jam without further damage and the Dodgers still led until the eighth. Forster was pitching when Blair singled and was sacrificed to second. Munson then drove a double down the third base line past Cey to drive in the tying run. Forster then fired a fastball which hit Reggie under the right elbow.

He hollered angrily at the pitcher before proceeding to first base. He said later, "I think they're throwing inside on me, thinking if it hits me it's all right, it's better than letting him hit. Well, it's not right and I don't like it."

Welch came in to pop up Piniella and strike out Nettles, though Graig, who'd made another remarkable lunging backhanded grab of a liner by Lopes in the third, hooked a "homer" just foul before fanning.

Gossage came in to match fastballs with Welch through the ninth and tenth. In the tenth, Welch walked White. With two out, Jackson came up to face Welch in a dramatic rematch of their second-game duel. This time, Reggie ripped the rookie for a single that put White in scoring position. And Piniella scored him with a single that ended the tense contest, 4–3, and evened the series.

"We're on our way now," Reggie remarked later. Privately he told a friend, "We've broken their hearts."

It looked like that in Sunday afternoon's fifth game as the Dodgers fell apart. Lopes singled in the first and third and scored on hits by Smith and Russell off Beattie to give the visitors a 2–0 lead, but they did little right after that.

Hooten and his successors were ripped for 18 hits, 17 of them singles. Munson, Rivers, Doyle, and Dent had three hits each. Munson drove in five runs. White had two hits and drove in three runs. Jackson had one hit and failed to drive in a run, but at one point the

213

Dodgers declined to pitch to him with two men in scoring position and intentionally walked him.

Russell was charged with only one error, but made several other misplays. Smith and Garvey also were charged with errors, but the team made many more misplays. The Dodgers made mental as well as physical errors. They threw to the wrong bases at the wrong times. The Dodgers seemed defeated as they headed home, down by three victories to two.

They were. It was Hunter versus Sutton in the sixth game, but Sutton did not last long, while Hunter went seven strong innings and Gossage closed out the contest. Lopes, Dodger MVP of the Series, hit another homer to put the Dodgers in front early. But the Yankees took the lead in the second and never were headed after that.

Nettles singled and Spencer walked. Doyle doubled in one run, the first extra-base hit and first RBI of his brief big league career. Then dangerous Dent singled in two runs. In the sixth, Piniella singled and scored on a single by Doyle. Sutton left with a six-game World Series record of 10 runs allowed. Welch arrived. Dent then singled Doyle home.

In the seventh, Jackson faced Welch once again and won once again. He hit a two-run home run that carried so far to right that he, as he so often did, watched it go out with awe and admiration, jumping up and down a little in joy, before running it out.

Smiling the smile of a champion, Reggie Jackson celebrates
his second straight World Series victory in two years with the
New York Yankees and fifth in his incredible career. Thurman
Munson, not exactly Reggie's best buddy, looks at "Mr. October" with awe and admiration as a reporter looks in between
the two and a telecaster's microphone captures the hero's historic words.   *(Wide World Photos)*

This stretched his World Series hitting streak to 10 straight games. It also drove the final nail in the Dodger coffin, 7–2.

With the last out, the Yankees, "The Comeback Kings," who had completed "the miracle of 1978," raced delightedly off the field and into another champagne celebration in their clubhouse. Meanwhile 55,985 disappointed Dodger fans watched their heroes walk sadly away, defeated for the second straight World Series.

Lasorda lowered his head and wept in the Dodger dressing room. After a while he spoke of Nettles' superb plays and the play in which Jackson was hit by a throw as those that turned the tide against his team. But the Dodgers' big hitters had not hit in this Series. Lopes led with seven runs batted in, but five came in the first game. Smith and Cey each hit one big home run and little else. Garvey did not drive in a run.

Meanwhile, the Yankees set six-game World Series records with 68 hits and a .306 team batting average. Dent had 10 hits and Jackson nine. Doyle hit .438, Dent .417, and Jackson .391. Jackson led both teams in RBIs with eight, while Dent and Munson each drove in seven. The eighth and ninth hitters in the batting order, Doyle and Dent each had three hits in each of the last two games. Dent was named MVP of the Series.

Well, he was the surprise star from the playoff game

with the Red Sox on. He said, "I'm thrilled, but I think it should have been Nettles." It could have been Jackson for the third time. Once again he had come through in the clutch as no other player could. In the midst of the celebration in the Yankee dressing room, someone asked him how he felt to have been an important part of another championship, maybe the most important.

"It's nice of you to say so, but I don't know about that," he said. "I know I was an important part of it. I take pride in having been a part of five championship clubs in my career, Catfish and I. I don't think many players have been a part of so many. Maybe some of the old Yankees, but not many others."

He looked over at George Steinbrenner, who was being interviewed. "That man made it possible," he said. And then he looked over at Bob Lemon, who was being interviewed. "And that man," he said. Ironically, even as Lemon was speaking of what it was like to be fired in mid-season and wind up as manager of the world champions at the end of the season, his successor in Chicago, Doby, was being fired.

Jackson looked over at Thurman Munson, who was being interviewed, and said, "You don't have to be friends with a fellow to respect him. I respect him and he respects me. I respect all the players on this team and I think they all respect me now. He'll be back, I'll be back, we'll all be back unless we're traded.

We've come from so far back, from certain defeat so many times to win it all two times in a row that we deserve respect. We've been through so much together and won so much together, it would be sad to break us up now the way the A's broke up."

He sat on a chair, sagging a little, seeming to be bone-tired. He said, "I am tired. I'm thirty-two years old and I've been in the big leagues twelve years and I've played on five championship teams and I've been to hell and back. It takes a lot out of you. All the controversies and struggles take a lot out of you. It's not what it once was, but then I'm not what I once was, either. It's no longer a game and I'm no longer a boy.

"I've made mistakes and I've learned a lot of lessons in life. God has been good to me, I'm grateful, and all I want now is to live a good life. All I want now is to go home and sit down in some pretty place for about a month and watch the sun set each day. I'm happy to have come through when it counted and I'm happy we won and I just want to be left alone to enjoy it all for a little while."

A much misunderstood man, an emotional man who rode a roller coaster of emotions from day to day and year to year, he was, as always, an honest man, an outspoken man, a man who spoke too honestly at times, who acted impulsively at times, but who meant to harm no man and was at the heart of him a good man who was good to others.

Perhaps he took too much pride in his performances,

but he had earned that. He had been at his best when it meant the most, through stretch runs, not only the last two seasons, but for season after season before that with his other title teams. No player of his day had done as much when it meant as much, and this is what made him the truest of superstars.

He had 27 hits in pennant playoffs and 31 in World Series, 58 in all, which was the most of any player since the playoffs started preceding World Series. He had hit .417 and .333 in different playoffs and .450, .391, and .360 in different World Series. His .360 career average was the fourth highest in history for any player who had played in at least 20 World Series games. He had played in 24.

He had five home runs in playoffs and nine in the World Series, 14 in all. His nine in the World Series was sixth highest in history, and those who had hit more played in many more games. He had driven in a record 15 runs in playoffs and 23 in World Series, 38 in all, another record for the combined classics. He had driven in runs in nine of his last 10 World Series games, another record.

Others called him "Mr. October" now, but that was too limiting. It didn't take in September. Or August. He was, more than anything else, a man for all seasons.

Index

Index

Index